47F

THE WINES OF BURGUNDY

BY THE SAME AUTHORS

A Book of Burgundy : Pictures and Comments on the Wines of Burgundy (London, Lund Humphries, 1958) *(Out of Print)*.

The Wines of Burgundy, The English Edition of the present book (Paris, Presses Universitaires de France, 1974, 4th Edition).

Die Weine Burgunds, The German Edition of the present book (Paris, Presses Universitaires de France, 1976, 2nd Edition).

Japanese Edition of this Book (Tokyo, 1976).

BY PIERRE POUPON

Pensées d'un dégustateur (Nuits-Saint-Georges, Confrérie des Chevaliers du Tastevin, 1957).

Vignes et Jours. A Burgundian's Notebook (Beaune, Imprimerie Jean Dupin, 1963), Literary prize « Bourgogne 1963 ».

Toute la Bourgogne. Portrait d'une province (Paris, Presses Universitaires de France, 1970).

Plaisirs de la dégustation (Paris, Presses Universitaires de France, 1973).

Nouvelles pensées d'un dégustateur (Nuits-Saint-Georges, Confrérie des Chevaliers du Tastevin, 1974).

Chapter « La Bourgogne », in the *Guide des Vins et des Vignobles de France* (Brussels, Kressmann & Elsevier Sequoia editions, 1975).

Chapter « Vignes et vignerons de Bourgogne », in *Le Vin de Bourgogne* (Paris, Editions Montalba, 1976).

Mes Dégustations littéraires (Nuits-Saint-Georges, Confrérie des Chevaliers du Tastevin, 1979).

La Route des Vins de Bourgogne (Rennes, Ouest-France, 1984).

BY PIERRE POUPON AND SYLVAIN PITIOT

Les Grands Vignobles de Bourgogne (Paris, coll. « Le Grand Bernard des Vins de France », 1985).

BY PIERRE FORGEOT

Guide de l'Amateur de Bourgogne (Presses Universitaires de France, 1967) *(Out of Print)*.

Les contes de mon tastevin (Printed by the Author, 1968) *(Out of Print)*.

Chapter « Les vins de Bourgogne », in *Le grand livre du vin* (Lausanne, Edita 1969).

Pèlerinage aux sources du bourgogne (Colmar-Ingersheim, S.A.E.P., 1971).

Beaune, en Bourgogne (Colmar-Ingersheim, S.A.E.P., 1972).

Origine du vignoble bourguignon (1972).

PIERRE POUPON   **&**   **PIERRE FORGEOT**

Grand Officier du Tastevin   *Chevalier dans l'Ordre National*
Compagnon du Beaujolais   *du Mérite*
                 Grand Officier du Tastevin
                 Chevalier du Mérite Agricole

THE WINES
OF
BURGUNDY

DRAWINGS BY PAUL DEVAUX

Translated from the French by

EDWARD OTT   **&**   **MICHAEL OTT**

Chevalier du Mérite Agricole   *Diplômé de Spécialisation Viticole et Œnologique*
Chevalier du Tastevin   *de l'Ecole Régionale de Viticulture de Beaune*
                  Chevalier du Tastevin

EIGHTH EDITION, REVISED & BROUGHT UP TO DATE BY
LOUIS-RÉGIS AFFRE
and
CÉCILE PICARD

PRESSES UNIVERSITAIRES DE FRANCE
1987

The First Edition of this book
was awarded the literary prize
of the « Confrérie des Chevaliers du Tastevin »
in 1952

ISBN 2 13 041694 2
Dépôt légal — 1re édition : 1964

8e édition : 1987, novembre

© Presses Universitaires de France, 1964
108, boulevard Saint-Germain, 75006 Paris

CONTENTS

Chapter III

THE WINE

Chapter IV

THE APPELLATIONS OF ORIGIN IN BURGUNDY

CHAPTER V

THE CHARACTERISTICS OF THE WINES

CHAPTER VI

EAUX-DE-VIE AND SPARKLING WINES

CHAPTER VII

THE WINE TRADE

Chapter VIII

THE WINE CELLAR AND THE TABLE

Chapter IX

WINE FESTIVITIES

THE COMPLETE LIST OF CONTROLLED APPELLATIONS IN BURGUNDY

LIST OF CONTROLLED APPELLATIONS IN BURGUNDY

CHAPTER I

VITICULTURAL BURGUNDY

A) *Introduction*

The tourist who starts from Paris or Northern Europe and plans to travel down to the Côte d'Azur or the Alps and Italy by car would be well-advised to take the Route Nationale 6 because it runs the full length of "friendly and wine-loving Burgundy ; this countryside of good living and happy souls where the towns even have vine branches emblazoned on their Coats of Arms".

But, after skirting the Morvan forests and the length of the meadows of the River Saône and had the good fortune to appreciate a good bottle of wine in one of the inns or restaurants along the way, the traveller will probably be surprised, on arriving at Lyons, that he has not driven through a vast vineyard area.

The reason is, that before Burgundy became a viticultural area, it was geographically on a direct route between North and South. There are a number of routes which cut across the region, such as the Yonne-Canal waterway of Bourgogne Saône, the main railway line Paris-Dijon-Lyon-Marseille, the Route Nationale No. 6 and now the fast A.6 Motorway. They all naturally slip through the valleys which run alongside or skirt a multitude of foothills which lead to the Massif Central.

So if the traveller wishes to find the Burgundian vineyards, he must resist the inclination to follow the main road and branch off towards the hills. Here the vines hang back on the east or southeast facing slopes to enjoy the full strength of the sun. They surround the villages, encroach on waste land and rocks and even take a strangle-hold on the country paths which try to deprive them of their precious soil.

Our tourist will have been inspired if he leaves the main roads around Auxerre. By doing this, he will not miss his entrance to the vineyards of Burgundy. He should then make his way to Chablis which will be a good introduction to the picturesque viticultural villages. Afterwards he should go to Dijon *via* Tonnerre and Montbard, then strike south again. His attention will then be attracted on the right by a belt of vineyards spread out on the hillsides, exposed to the rising sun like a huge carpet which changes colour with the seasons. For nearly 125 miles and as far as the outskirts of Lyons, the vine does not leave the scene.

The first 30 miles of road from Dijon to Chagny unfolds along the very foot of the famous Côte d'Or, like a glorious avenue where one comes across all the nobility of the great growths. The Mercurey region starts a little further along in the Saône-et-Loire and continues to run beside the National 6 or the Motorway.

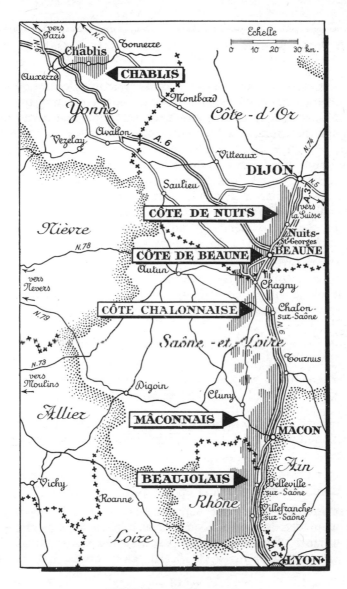

Viticultural Burgundy

The hills are no longer in a straight line formation and slope down quite appreciably as one winds one's way towards the Mâconnais. A closely knit network of narrow roads pass through peaceful villages, nearly all endowed with churches of a classical Romanesque style. Here the vine tries to make more and more inroads into the country. It encircles and swamps one on all sides. But it is in Beaujolais, in the Rhône Department that it reigns supreme, coming right down to the banks of the Saône. It occupies all the available ground and climbs the steep slopes of an almost mountainous district before it is barred to the west by the Beaujolais hills where the average altitude exceeds 2,000 feet.

What a greeting the traveller will give all these vines! What joy he will have travelling through the area and admiring the view ; how eager he will be when finally guided into the depths of a large cellar or the darkness of a small one to taste any of these wines of Burgundy which are now the delight of the entire world.

B) *Delimitation*

The whole of the Burgundy vineyards, producing controlled appellation wines (A.O.C.) is officially described as Viticultural Burgundy.

VITICULTURAL BURGUNDY was defined by a judgment of the Civil Tribunal of Dijon on the 29th April 1930.

It stretches over four departments. A table below shows the main details for each one. It also gives an indication of the number of vines in the departments producing wines for current consumption (V.C.C.). In other words, not having the right to the Controlled Appellation of Origin. They only account for a small proportion and are mentioned here for comparison.

Departments	Number of harvest declarations	Area of production (in hectares)	Harvest A.O.C. wines in 1986 (in hectolitres)	
			White	Red
Yonne	3,764	2,749	155,225	21,468
Côte-d'Or..........	7,311	7,479	103,057	339,837
Saône-et-Loire.......	11,860	8,206	277,884	362,080
Rhône	14,451	19,734	3,933	1,277,718
TOTAL	37,386	38,168	540,099	2,001,103

The department of the YONNE includes *the region of Chablis* which specialises in the production of well known white wines. Here, this small vineyard area of rolling hills consists of less than twenty communes where agriculture is as important as viticulture.

The department of the CÔTE-D'OR comprises :

— To the north, *The Côte de Nuits*, where the celebrated Crus principally come from : Gevrey-Chambertin, Morey-Saint-Denis, Chambolle-Musigny, Vougeot, Vosne-Romanée, Nuits-Saint-Georges (see p. 105);

— To the south, *The Côte de Beaune*, which produces in addition to great red wines, the best white wines in Burgundy. It stretches from Aloxe-Corton to Santenay passing through Savigny-lès-Beaune, Pernand-Verge-lesses, Beaune, Pommard, Volnay, Monthelie, Auxey-

Duresses, Saint-Romain, Meursault (capital of the great white wines), Puligny-Montrachet, Chassagne-Montrachet, etc. (see p. 127).

The department of SAÔNE-ET-LOIRE comprises :

— To the north, *the region of Mercurey* (Rully, Givry, Montagny), connected traditionally to the Côte-d'Or (see p. 166).
— To the south, *the Mâconnais*, a vast vineyard divided into a number of communes, producing red and more particularly white wines. The villages producing the best quality white wines are Vergisson, Solutré, Pouilly, Fuissé and Chaintré (see p. 170).

Finally, the department of the RHÔNE, comprises *the Beaujolais* where the vineyards stretch as far as Chapelle-de-Guinchay to the north in the department of the Saône-et-Loire and, in the south, they encroach on the outskirts of Villefranche-en-Beaujolais and, even, several villages very close to Lyon (see p. 175).

Referring to Beaujolais, people frequently ask the question — "Is Beaujolais really a part of Burgundy ?" A clear answer must be given here once and for all. From an historic point of view, Beaujolais has never belonged to the province of Burgundy, but always to that of Lyon. On the other hand, from a geographical point of view, Beaujolais appears quite naturally to be linked with the Burgundian country. Its vineyards are closely attached to those of the Mâconnais and are also planted on hillsides which face the east on the plain of the Saône. In addition, from a trade point of view, the wines from Beaujolais are, to a great extent, marketed by the wine merchants of the Mâconnais and the Côte-d'Or. Finally, the vine variety of Beaujolais, the Gamay is so typically Burgundian that in the Middle Ages, it became necessary to destroy the Pinot on the hillsides of Nuits and Beaune. Also, the nine best Crus to which it gave birth have the right to change their appellation of origin to that of "Bourgogne".

C) *Origins*

It has needed several centuries of hard, eager work to hang up at the back of these slopes "the tightly knit curtain of vineyards" which to-day enriches the cradle of one of the most beautiful glories and one of the greatest Ambassadors of France : "MONSEIGNEUR LE VIN DE BOURGOGNE".

The art of pruning and cultivating the vine goes back far into history, but it was principally the Greeks and Romans who were noted for their craftsmanship. In what circumstances, by which route, and at what moment did this art manage to reach Gaul, where Burgundy is situated to-day ? Historians and archaeologists are always in dispute over the facts. But little does it matter to us. The main point is to know that the Burgundian civilisation of the vine began at the dawn of our era and developed during the sixth century when Burgundy saw the birth of a number of monastries, whose viticultural work was remarkable.

"*No province*, wrote Michelet, *had larger abbeys which were more rich, more prolific, in far off colonies : Saint-Bénigne at Dijon; near Mâcon, Cluny; and Cîteaux, two steps from Chalon.*"

The monks of Cîteaux started the celebrated wines of Burgundy in the xIIth century, after bringing the land back into cultivation and planting vines in ground received from donations.

The fame of these wines was subsequently backed and spread by the Court of the Dukes of Burgundy. They finally reached the attention of Louis XIV, thanks to his doctor Fagon, who recommended the wines of the Côte-d'Or to him. Their fame was also spread by the Beaujolais vinegrower Claude Brosse who took his harvest as far as Verseilles, where it had the good fortune to be commented upon by the King.

The name was "launched" ; demand followed and business began. At the beginning of the xvIIIth century the first firms were founded in Beaune and the wine merchants first of all visited the north of France, and Belgium which formerly belonged to the ancient Duchy of Burgundy and was already appreciative of the quality of the products offered. Shortly other firms were started in Nuits and Dijon. At the end of the xvIIIth century, the French Revolution triggered off the dispersal of the large estates belonging to the nobility and religious orders. Properties were broken up and the situation was later aggravated by families dividing their land. Today these divisions remain and are still one of the main weaknesses and a characteristic of the Burgundian vineyard. From the xIXth century the sale of Burgundian wines made great progress and exporting was rapidly becoming one of the principle outlets. As fast as land and maritime transport developed, England, Ireland and then Belgium, the Scandinavian countries, Switzerland, followed by Germany and finally other overseas markets were being counted, by degrees, as traditional importers of these wines.

D) *The Phylloxera Crisis*

All civilisations are mortal, and, like many others, that of the vine nearly succumbed towards 1878 under the crafty invasion of phylloxera since nicknamed "vastatrix" or, in other words, "ravager".

In the Gard area of France, attention was drawn in 1863 to this formidable insect of American origin. In 1866 it was at Orange ; in 1867 in the Vaucluse ; in 1868 in the Drôme. It attacked Villié-Morgon (Beaujolais) in 1874, arriving near Tournus in 1875, seizing Meursault, capital of the great white wines and bastion of the Côte de Pourpre et d'Or, in 1878. This advance was a succession of terrible disasters for the French vineyards. Was our country going to be deprived of its most basic product ? The sight of devasted hillsides, dried up cellars, ruined villages, was haunting the nights of the vine-grower. Were the rich slopes of the Côte-d'Or to become the meagre pastures for sheep ? It was when Stendhal, quite rightly this time, could have said, as he wrote in 1837 that this hillside was "no more than a little mountain truly dry and ugly".

But the Comités de Vigilance were facing up to the danger and finally succeeded not only in halting the phylloxera but in neutralising it.

They were, in fact, discovering that these insects were not causing any damage to American plants and they therefore advocated the grafting of the French vines on to the American stock, preaching as far back as 1866 the crusade of the reconstruction of the vineyards.

At the turn of the century the distress caused by this pest was no more than a bad memory already being forgotten.

In spite of this deadly menace and even actually during the phylloxera invasion, the wines of Burgundy maintained their reputation by the great vintages of 1881, 1885, 1886, 1887, 1894 and 1898. After the reconstruction of the vineyards the fine years 1904, 1906, 1911, 1915 and 1919 proved to the whole world that their wines coming from grafted stock had not lost any of their merits or their qualities.

To-day, the scientific progress and modern equipment used in viticulture and œnology permit these wines to maintain their high ranking qualities.

Chapter II

THE VINE

1. THE LIFE AND CULTURE OF THE VINE

A) *The Bush*

The vine (of the *vitis* species in botany) is a plant of the *ampelideae* family. It grows essentially in hot or temperate regions and consists of a great number of varieties amongst which the *vitis vinifera* is included. It provides all the vine plants used in Europe and notably in Burgundy.

The vine is a climbing and shooting bush of which the main organs are :

— *the roots,* which support the plant, have a respiratory and nutritive function and carry the sap ;

— *the stock* (the foot of the vine) which bears the shoots or canes ;

— *the canes,* on which one finds small swellings in tiers : the nodes ;

— *the nodes*, which give birth to buds for future shoots, leaves, tendrils (supporting organs) and finally bunches of grapes ;

— *the buds*, which are of several types, but the principal ones develop into branches or canes ;

— *the leaves*, carry out a respiratory and nutritive function, and, assisted by sunlight, transform the sap into the necessary elements to make grapes ;

— *the fruit*, in the form of berries are joined together into bunches : the grapes.

B) *The Biological Cycle*

The life of the vine starts at the end of the winter with the first of the year's sunshine. At the end of the canes, pruned by secateurs, appear sparkling drops. These are the *tears* of the vine, tears of joy, from the old stock awakened by the thrust of new sap.

Next, the buds swell with a rise in temperature (about 10 ºC) and, with humidity, open, throwing off their bud scales (known as *bud burst*) and soon sprinkle the vineyards with tender little green leaves, in the middle of which can be seen minute bunches of grapes. The *leafing starts* quite slowly but accelerates as soon as the growth warms up. In effect, it is this rapid growth of the vine which sometimes falls victim to spring frosts. Intoxicated by the warmth, the leafy branches stretch out undisciplined and choking.

Then comes the flowering (early June) when the temperature reaches an average of 20 ºC. "*The vine in flower exhales*, wrote Roupnel, *an embalmed breath, as if it was the lily and the rose of all the land*". Suddenly calmed, the vine requires at the time of *pollination*, long days of sunshine. The berry starts to take shape (setting), already nourishing itself and rapidly gaining in weight and size. At the height of development, it changes from a green colour to a transparent yellow or a deep violet depending on the type of vine. This process is known as *véraison*; supplied by the roots and leaves, the grape fills up with sugar until it can absorb no more. *The maturity of the fruit* is now complete and all that remains is for it to be picked; in other words, the vintage has arrived.

The maturing of the wood *(lignification)* and the grapes, takes place at the same time. The canes seem to dry out but, in point of fact, they are storing nourishment which will be used to feed the buds in the coming spring, and which are now being rejected by the grapes. At the end of October, or beginning of November, the leaves turn yellow and red, clothing the vineyards for several days with sumptuously rich colours.

When the cold weather starts, the leaves fall and the vines are reduced to a skeleton-like state ready for their half-dead world of hibernation.

C) *Calendar of Vineyard Work*

Preliminary remarks : most of the work which used to call for the physical effort of men and horses has been replaced by tractors. General mechanisation has spread slowly through the vineyards, alleviating fatigue and gaining time. So the work and life of the grower in the last quarter of the xxth century has no longer anything in common with his work and life in 1950.

OCTOBER

— *end of the harvest;*

— *trench ploughing,* or preparation of soil for ploughing or replanting. Aim : breaking up and clearing of ground and pulling out degenerated roots. This job is carried out by a special plough (trench plougher) pulled by a winch or a tractor. Generally speaking, trench ploughing is finished by deep manuring and disinfecting. In Burgundy, the depth of the trench is between 16 and 19 inches.

NOVEMBER

— *trench ploughing;*

— *preparatory pruning (épondage)* : with the help of the "coupe souche", large secateurs with long handles, one cuts the fruit branches and takes off useless shoots at the base of the vine. All is now ready for the spring pruning;

— *cane burning* : a short time ago, the collecting of canes was a long and tedious job. It consisted of bundling the cut branches together and taking them on one's back to the edge of the vineyard where they were burnt in a pile. To-day, this work is made much easier by the use of a special wheelbarrow for burning the branches. The branches are cut and put into a wheelbarrow which has been specially converted to contain a burner. The vinegrower pushes the burner along as he works and burns the branches at the same time. It also warms him and keeps him company;

— *hilling-up :* this is a job which should normally be completed before the very cold weather. The object is to prepare the soil which will be broken up by the winter frosts and to protect the base of the vines against these frosts;

— *soil replacement :* in certain sloping vineyards which are subject to water erosion, the vines situated at the top are deprived of soil at the expense of those lower down. It is therefore necessary to replace the soil at the top.

DECEMBER

— *trench ploughing;*
— *preparatory pruning or "épondage"* (except in frosty weather);
— *cane burning;*
— *hilling up;*
— *soil replacement.*

JANUARY

— *pruning* (but it is preferable to wait until the following month). In Burgundy, tradition dictates that pruning never starts before St. Vincent's day on the 22nd January—the fête of the vinegrowers.

FEBRUARY

— *pruning*. Object : to direct, regulate and improve the vegetation and fruiting of the vine.

Pruning is an important and delicate operation calling for judgment and observation. In the first place there are several principles to be followed according to the system adopted and depending on the type of vine, soil and climate. But the vinegrower also finds himself faced with a number of particular cases which he must work out to the rhythm of his pruning scissors. Each vine poses a problem which he must not only solve by using his common sense, but also by taking into consideration certain data such as the abundance of shoots, the age of the vine, its plantation density ; results of past yields, meteorological accidents or diseases from which it may have suffered. Left entirely to nature the vine becomes tangled up with useless branches which quickly exhaust it and hinder regular fruiting. One must, therefore, domesticate the vine like an animal. Olivier de Serres whose *Théâtre d'Agriculture* is the peasant's and vinegrower's bible, wrote concerning pruning that *One must not let the vine have its own way any more than one would let a young strong horse.*

Pruning calls for a lot of practice and only the vinegrower who halts several times a year and over a number of years in front of each of his vines, can, if he loves his craft, acquire sufficient experience to enable him to guide the vine with perfection. Pruning is the work of craftsmen against which this mechanical civilisation will always remain powerless.

Here the machine will never be able to replace the brain and hands of man.

In Beaujolais, they usually use the gobelet method of pruning. The vine is cut quite low leaving three or four arms which bear the renewal spurs, pruned to two buds. There is no tying up except in young vines where the shoots are still too weak to hold themselves erect; these are attached to stakes.

In the Mâcon district they use the tailed pruning which consists of two shoots being bent over to form an arch on each side of the vine; the ends are attached to the lowest wire of the trellis-work.

The most common method of pruning found in the Côte-d'Or is the *"Guyot" cordon*. The vine is kept quite low to the ground, only two branches being retained each year; one is the fruit cane which is bent to about a foot from the soil, fixed horizontally along the lowest wire and pruned back to several buds giving the fruit branches. The other is the "renewal spur" pruned leaving two buds; these will produce the replacement branches for the following year. Formerly stakes were used for tying up but now three wires (the middle one being double) lying one above the other and supported by stakes, have taken their place.

For several years, the Institute National des Appellations d'Origine has undertaken trials with another type of training called "Vignes Hautes" in the Côte-d'Or. This new method of training is characterised by the vines being grown to a greater height and being widely spaced. The advantages of this method are that it encourages a healthier cultivation, reduces operational costs and, above all, cuts down the amount of pruning.

The recent decree of the 24th July 1982 limits the productions of this type of vines called "hautes" and "larges" to two appellations : Bourgogne Hautes-Côtes de Beaune and Bourgogne Hautes-Côtes de Nuits. This same decree prohibits the cultivation of "vignes hautes" to other appellations in particular the appellation Bourgogne. However the vines planted before 1980 are allowed to stay until *time to pull up the vines by the roots.*

Finally, in the Yonne, the pruning is quite different. In effect they use cordon pruning but the length of the renewal spur is adapted to suit certain local conditions such as the slope and nature of the ground, age of the vine, etc. Another important characteristic is that the cordoning is generally directed towards the bottom of the slope ; contrary to practice elsewhere.

MARCH

— *transporting and spreading of fertilisers :* the vine requires nitrogen (for the vegetation), phosphoric acid (for fruiting and maintaining a good healthy state) and potassium (to increase the yield, giving the must more sugar and less acidity, also giving greater resistance to disease and frosts). Manure is always the best fertiliser because it produces humus. But it is becoming difficult to find and the growers now principally use other organic or general purpose fertilisers following advice given by Agricultural Advisory Boards.

— *pruning;*

— *ploughing back :* as the name implies, ploughing back is the opposite of hilling up. It consists of freeing the vines from soil which covers their bases. This job evenly distributes and airs the soil, broken up by the cold weather during the winter. It also allows the use of fertilisers. At the same time, young weeds are destroyed and larvae are killed by exposing them to the cold.

— *grafting :* since the phylloxera outbreak, grafting has been used for the propagation of the vine. By joining a scion (cane selected to provide the required grape variety) on to a stock (cane of an American vine which is immune to phylloxera punctures), a graft is obtained. This is placed in sand or white wood sawdust in a temperature of 20 ºC. The union should be completed by the end of two or three weeks.

Grafting is carried out on a bench in a workroom with the aid of a grafting knife or even a grafting machine. The commonest graft is the "whip and tongue" which consists of cutting the scion and stock at the same angle and then splitting them so that they lock perfectly into each other.

— *bouéchage :* a Burgundian term derived from the verb *bêcher*, to dig. This manual work finishes or replaces ploughing in places where the plough cannot reach. It is carried out by using a sort of hoe which comes in many shapes. Now that weed killer is used, the main purpose is to remove any roots which are found to be growing where the stock and scion have been joined together.

P. POUPON AND P. FORGEOT
2

APRIL

— *ploughing back ;*

— *bouéchage ;*

— *cane burning ;*

— *fastening.* The fixing of fruit canes to the bottom wire which forms the horizontal cordon.

— *hoeing :* a superficial work which does the same job as harrowing, i.e. the destruction of weeds and breaking up of the crust formed on the surface of the soil. To-day, its main use is to dig in fertilisers which have been applied ;

— *planting :* the year-old grafts are uprooted from the nursery and trimmed (the roots are cut to between 4 and 6 inches), then planted in ground that thas been trench ploughed in the previous autumn, harrowed and marked out with stakes indicating where to plant the new vines.

From the "third leaf", in other words, the third year of plantation, a vine starts to produce a few grapes. After its fourth leaf (fourth year), the vine can already give an appreciable yield of fruit.

But it must not be overlooked that before planting a young vine in the place of an old one, the ground must be left fallow for two or three years and well manured. On average, a normal yield is not obtained until the sixth year or even the seventh.

MAY

— *application of weed-killer* : this is a new development. It consists of spraying the ground with chemical weed-killer which stops the weeds growing in the rows or kills them if they are already there. This seems the better method when the ground is sloping as it prevents the risk of disturbing the soil when thunder storms are encountered during the summer ;

— *planting the grafts in the nurseries* : the young grafts taken from the sand or wood sawdust (see p. 33) are planted in previously selected ground which has been prepared and manured. The nursery will then be under constant supervision such as watering, hoeing and various treatments ;

— *treatments* : the object is to protect the vine against a number of parasites, various insects and microscopic fungi responsible for well-known diseases such as downy mildew and oidium.

A short time ago, the only treatment against downy mildew was copper sulphate neutralised by lime. Sulphating consisted of spraying the vines with fine droplets containing the mixture from wide armed sprayers pulled by horses or tractors.

Sulphating has now been replaced nearly everywhere by synthetic fungicides and insecticides. These are applied by modern equipment attached to the tractor, allowing quick and controlled treatment. Sulphating by helicopter is undertaken but mainly where the soil has been softened by rain and made difficult for tractors to work.

It is advantageous to carry out the first treatment as early as possible, that is towards the end of the bud-burst. If the year is favourable to mildew, the treatments are used regularly up to the middle of July.

For a long time, the frequency and dates of these treatments were left to the hazardous decisions of the vinegrowers. But nowadays each viticultural area has an Agricultural Warning Station at its disposal which centralises information gathered from observation posts spread out over the vineyards. These recordings allow the Station to keep an eye on the evolution of diseases and to recommend appropriate cures immediately. In this way, the growers can treat their vines with maximum efficiency.

Treatments against mildew are frequently combined with those against Oidium (see p. 37) by the use of wettable sulphur, and against other enemies of the vineyard (mostly grape caterpillars) by phosphoric esters, etc.

— *de-suckering* (known in Burgundy as *évasivage* or *éjetonnement*) : removal of young green shoots which have developed on the plant and use sap required by the fruit branches ;

— *tying up :* this consists of pushing back into line those leafy branches which have spread out in all directions. They are secured between the double wire in the middle of the trellis ;

— *tying down :* fixing of branches on to one of the double wires.

Fastening, tying up and tying down are done so as to leave a clear passage between the rows for viticultural implements and tractors to pass. It also permits light to reach the young bunches of grapes. These jobs call for considerable additional labour so the growers call on their wives and daughters to assist them in this long and precise task. Tying material used to include rye straw, osiers and rushes. To-day, plastic or metal clips are used which are quick to apply.

JUNE

— *tying up and tying down ;*

— *treatments ;*

— *sulphuring* : treatment against Oidium. The most effective is powdered sulphur which acts as a deterrent. It is projected on to the vines by blowers. To obtain the best results, sulphuring should be done on a still morning when fine weather is forecast. The vapour given off by the sulphur combined with the action of heat (about 25 °C), checks oidium from developing. For the times and frequency of application, the grower can consult the Agricultural Warning Station in the same way as for sulphating.

The treatment with wettable sulphur (which works in cold wet conditions unlike powdered sulphur) is being used more and more as it can be combined with treatments against Mildew (see p. 35). But the Chardonnay vine is very sensitive to Oidium so at least one dressing must be made with powdered sulphur.

— *disinfecting the soil* : this is now a widespread practice. It consists of spraying the ground contaminated by virus infections with chemical products which purify the area. This work has to be done when the soil is well warmed and neither too dry or humid.

JULY

— *treatments ;*

— *hoeing ;*

— *bouéchage ;*

— *pinching back* (topping) : the ends of the leafy branches which are continually growing and absorbing quite a lot of nutritive matter destined to the grape, are pruned. This job carried out by hand shears is being replaced more and more by a tractor fitted with horizontal and vertical clippers.

AUGUST

— *pinching back ;*

— *miscellaneous maintenance :* repairs to enclosure walls, etc. ;

–– *nursing the grafts :* stopping roots from forming on the scion which should be growing on the stock ;

— *preparation of the wine-making equipment :* the first condition of a good vinification is to make certain that the materials to be used are clean and in working order. The tubs, casks and vats are cleaned and soaked to make certain the wood is watertight! Baskets, hose-pipes, presses, crushers and stemmers are also thoroughly cleaned. All iron parts are painted with spirit, varnish or a lacquer to prevent rusting and the contact of the must with metallic parts. Pumps and motors are cleaned, greased and tested. Plastics, enamelled and stainless steel have all made the task of cleaning far easier.

SEPTEMBER

— *miscellaneous maintenance;*
— *preparation of wine making equipment;*
— *harvesting :* these are the great days of Burgundy, the crowning of long months of work, the end of the viti-cultural year.

From the first glimmers of dawn, wrote Roupnel (1), *the village is humming like an apiary... And now, happy groups stride along all the roads. The men in their long sticky aprons, carrying on their shoulders piles of empty baskets. The women wear the white "capeline" on their heads carrying the "vendan-gerot" baskets on their arms. Trailing behind are already a few inattentive couples. Here are the gangs going to work! The "secateur" cuts the grapes. The "vendangerot" heaps them up. The small basket-emptier hopping about in the dew tips them up. On the Côte de Nuits, an almost square basket in used to collect this violet harvest. On the Côte de Beaune they use an oblong basket forming a waist at the handle. Further south, in the Chas-sagne district, they harvest with a basket carried on the back called "une hotte"... The men are busy emptying their baskets full of grapes into large "ballonges" (2)... Every evening, the*

(1) *La Bourgogne* (Horizons de France).
(2) An oval-shaped tub placed on a two-wheeled cart or a tractor-drawntrailer and serving as a transporter for about a ton of grapes from the vines to the cellar.

streets of the village are a tumult of carts and horses, cries and clamours... The bands of harvesters disperse and regroup as if they were trying to be everywhere at once... In the meantime, the "ballonges" are being emptied in the courtyards.

To-day, the harvesting teams are mainly made up of young students, French and foreign, who are attracted by the money and the folklore surrounding the work. As the students come from far and wide, the grower is compelled to organise food and lodging.

The harvest becoming too much of a costly task, the vinegrowers are considering the harvesting machine like a liberation. In 1984 some very satisfactory trials have been made on models adjusted by two industrials of the Côte de Beaune. The vinegrowers are eager to invest in this quite rapidly redeemable material.

The I.N.A.O. is studying carefully the consequences of this mechanical harvest on the quality of the wines and the I.N.A.O. made reserves in respect of the Beaujolais region where the grapes needs to be whole and intact to respect the norms for a good vinification.

Dates of the harvesting. — This date depends upon the state of ripeness of the grapes. Formerly, this was fixed by tasting the grapes. Local traditions were also followed. It was expected, for example, that the harvest could start one hundred days after the flowering of the lily. The *ban de vendange* which fixes the date from which gathering is permitted in each commune, was thus rigorously respected.

To-day, the trend is to determine scientifically the state of ripeness of the grape. That is to say, the moment at which the grape reaches its maximum development, containing the maximum sugar and minimum acidity. In practice, a musti-meter or refractometer is used every two or three days to record the sugar richness of the must. When the sugar content becomes more or less stable then the time to harvest has arrived.

This method is quite simple but not very precise. A more reliable method has been found in the laboratory which gene-rally speaking enables the date of harvesting to be predicted a few days in advance. After several samples from the grapes, followed by analysis of the must, it is possible to express gra-phically the development of the main constituents of the grape and to refer to a ripeness index. In this way, it is possible to forecast the actual date of maturity. The Œnological Stations publish the results of these analyses in the local press with comments to help and guide the growers.

These different methods can be unreliable if the sample has not been taken correctly, as not all of the vines are of the same age, have the same attention or are in the same vegetative state. It is therefore up to the grower who knows each plot inti-mately, to decide in the last resort.

2. THE ENEMIES OF THE VINE

Since the beginning of time, all vine-growers have been compelled to guard their vines against diseases and protect them from threatening enemies.

There is no end to either of them. If certain afflictions disappear there are always others to take their place. Today this situation still exists, in spite of the protection available and the advances of chemistry.

We will not look back retrospectively here nor shall we enumerate all the parasitic, cryptogamic, physiological and meteorological disasters of which the vine has been the victim down the ages. We shall be satisfied by only pointing out those which still arouse the Burgundian growers and which cause them considerable worry.

Leaving aside the always present phylloxera which is made harmless by the use of resistent vine-stocks, the attacks from parasitic insects are primarily the work of grape-worms and red spiders.

Grape caterpillars come from two moths, the Totrix moth and the Grape-berry moth, and they devour the floral buds of the grape bunches in the springtime or directly attack the grape-berries during the summer period.

Red spiders are tiny mites which have recently become harder to deal with because of their proliferation. They make numerous punctures in the leaves which weakens the vegetation and upsets the ripening of the grapes.

The damage caused by various fungi is always considerable because they provoke well known diseases such as Oidium and Downy Mildew. But today with modern techniques like synthetic organic products we cannot only check the diseases but prevent them. In spite of all this, it is a constant struggle. The grower who disregards a certain treatment or gives it too late may see his harvest waste away or disappear due to the grapes failing to develop.

Grey-rot is likewise caused by a fungus. In some years its effects can be checked. Although when the humidity is at its greatest in August and September, the growers still do not have a really effective way of dealing with the problem.

In fact virus and not moulds are the carriers of a group of diseases classified under the general heading of "infectious degenerative diseases". The most widespread and disturbing of these degenerators in Burgundy is the Court-Noué (literally the short knotted), so named because the internodes become shorter and shorter. The Court-Noué becomes evident by the appearance of a number of abnormalities, which wither and often kill the entire vine. The grower is still powerless when faced with this virus. There is only one drastic course of action to take to destroy it, up-root the vine in question, disinfect and cleanse the soil, then replant with healthy stocks and scions.

Besides these attacks, by insects, moulds and virus which together come to destroy the health of the vine and upset the fruiting, the future vintage is the whole time threatened by the whims of the weather, cold, frost, fog, rain, storms and hail. The vine is also extremely sensitive to even slight changes in climatic conditions. It is not only the winter and spring frost which can freeze the vine to death and destroy the young buds, but equally harmful are ordinary periods of cold and rain, especially if they come at the time of flowering in June. They can cause "coulure" or "millerandage" which have the power to reduce a harvest by an appreciable amount, by aborting the flowers, or leaving the pollination incomplete. Hail, which fortunately only strikes a small area at any one time has the violence and cruelty of point-blank rifle fire, nothing can resist it. Delicate branches, shoots, leaves and grapes are unable to withstand it. Alas, the vine-grower in spite of all his ingenuity is still very badly equipped to protect his livelihood against all these meteorological misfortunes. But, is the day really far off when man can be master of his climate ?

Waiting for this day to arrive, the grower makes use of modern technics to protect his vines. In Burgundy, we have seen, during the past few years, various ways to fight the frost in the most susceptible areas. Special candles and burners, run on gas or oil, are occasionally placed in the vineyards at night to heat the air. But there is room for improvement as the present methods are difficult to operate effectively.

The protection against hail is generally by the use of aeroplanes which sprinkle the suspected clouds with millions of silver iodide particles, stopping the formation of the devasting hailstones.

Aeroplanes and helicopters can again help the grower when treatments need to be undertaken especially where the plots are difficult to work.

3. CRAFTSMEN OF THE QUALITY

The vine produces grapes and the juice from these grapes has the property of transforming itself into wine. Up to that point there are no mysteries that have not been explained. Botanists tell us in detail about the biography of the vine and œnologists are slowly finding out about the intricacies of fermentation.

But there is another mystery ; that of quality, its complexities resist the most patient scientists in the same way as the character of a man outstrips the observations of the psychologist. Is it not equally as difficult to try to explain the character of an individual as it is to explain the quality of a wine ? One will never know the precise causes of this phenomenon as the factors which make up quality are so numerous and varied. However, certain data found in each case, can be relied on, bringing us nearer to the solution. There is the well-known theory that Taine used to justify the qualities of a work. It claimed that because the author belonged to a "race", to an "environment" and to a given "moment" he was fated to write the work concerned.

We will make this our theory, somewhat roughly defined but nevertheless suitably applied to try and analyse the principle elements which make up "the master mind" of the wines of Burgundy ; in other words, their quality.

The "race" is the vineplant, a known type of the vegetable species *vitis vinifera*. The "environment" is the soil ; that parcel of land where the vine grows. The "moment" is the site, the meteorological circumstances in which the vineplant finds itself involved. Finally, there is the birth of the wine through its vinification. But, however well designed the pre-determined theories are, there are always the "imponderable" elements which occasionally make these theories go wrong.

Let us then look at these craftsmen of quality one by one, these magicians who bring their gifts to the wine that is preparing to be born.

A) The Vineplant

Since the phylloxera crisis (see p. 23), the native vine has made use of the roots of a hardy foreign stock to protect and nourish it and has still retained the characteristics which it had before.

Let us point out at once that the list of vines do not correspond to a strict botanical uniformity but to individual groups (vine plants) which have a certain number of visible characteristics in common. (The leaf formation in particular.) Comparing them has shown their differences in quality and quantity performance. Clonal selection (starting from a vine plant) has become a way of improving the varieties and encouraging results have been obtained.

Since about 1960 Burgundy has been doing important research on the selection of the varieties and sanitation of the wine. This is how the winegrowers can now plant grafts of clones with the label "certified material". This means the performances have been observed in experimental vineyards regarding the vegetative behavior of the vine and the quality of the wines obtained. The planting of two or three different clones in the same vineyard allows for the realisation of a harmonious combination of their complementary performances.

To avoid entering into too much detail and special cases, we shall only distinguish between four main types of Burgundian vine : the Pinot, the Gamay, the Chardonnay and the Aligoté.

The Pinot has made the reputation of these great red wines ever since the creation of the Burgundian vineyards. It produces compact bunches of fine purplish-blue-black coloured grapes whose tight little berries contain plenty of clear, sugary juice.

The thick leaves are a dull dark green on the upper side and a clear green on the underside, being as broad as they are long and divided into three or five lobes, their size depending on the vine's fertility. It must be emphasised that the juice of the Pinot grape is colourless. This is why when vinified in a special way the same juice coming from the same vine makes Champagne. In Burgundy, it is at the time of fermentation in vat that the colouring matter contained in the grape skin gives the wine its pretty red tint.

Fine claims to fame for this vine of noble race which gives birth to the great "crus" of the Côte-d'Or and Champagne, at one and the same time.

The Gamay has borrowed its name from a hamlet lying in the vicinity of Puligny-Montrachet, and is mentioned in several texts from the xivth century. It is quite a fruitful plant of which the grapes are more or less compact depending upon the variety. The vine that interests us here is the *Gamay noir à jus blanc* which on the granite hillsides of Beaujolais produces pleasant *red wines* having a good nose, but when planted in the clayey limestone of Burgundy only makes the more ordinary types of wines. Beaujolais and Mâcon owe their reputation to this grape.

The Chardonnay has also been a Burgundian plant for centuries. The *great white wines* of the Côte-d'Or (Montrachet, Meursault, etc.), the first white growths of Mercurey (Rully) and the Mâcon area (Pouilly-Fuissé), also the wines of Chablis in the Yonne where it is locally known as the *Beaunois*, are proof of its quality. It produces pretty golden bunches as small as the Pinot variety but longer and far less compact. The berries are small but rich in white juice, deliciously sugared. Its leaves are recognised by two large nervures borde-ring the opening of the tail (stalk sinus).

The Aligoté is a semi-choice vine which has been grown in Burgundy for a very long time, it is quite a strong plant. Its white grapes are larger and more numerous than those of the Chardonnay, consequently the yield is greater.

This vine is grown nearly everywhere in soil that is not suitable for the Pinot and Chardonnay but which is never-theless still excellent soil for vines. The wine that it produces is not entitled to carry the name of the village where the vine has been cultivated but has to be called "Bourgogne Aligoté". It is also used considerably in the making of Sparkling Burgundy.

Several other types of vine of lesser importance are found in the Chablis region, notably the Sauvignon and the César. The first one produces a V.D.Q.S. called "Sauvignon de Saint-Bris" and, the second, connected to the Pinot gives strength and keeping power to a Burgundy coming from the vineyards of Irancy, to the South of Auxerre.

But it is not enough just to select a good vine to obtain a quality wine, the correct method of pruning must be used for each variety and a site must be found where the vine will have a chance to fruit under the best conditions.

B) **The soil**

Generally speaking, the vine prefers stony ground which drains and warms up easily. One will generally find it in ground composed of silica (light wine), clay (coloured, alcoholic, coarse and tannic wines), limestone (alcoholic and perfumed wines) and iron oxide (coloured and perfumed wines).

Composition of a few soils according to different authors

Growths	Silica	Clay	Limestone	Iron oxide
	%	%	%	%
Clos-de-Vougeot	47.1	36.7	12	3.2
Moulin-à-vent	81.6	3.03	0.9	11.3
Montrachet	33.7	28.1	31.6	

In Beaujolais the soil on the slopes is granite, schistous and clayish without limestone ; that of the low lying land is marly, heavier, damper and sometimes lightened by traces of limestone.

The vineyards of the Maconnais are spread over a large area and consist of a variety of soils. In the South, they are like those in Beaujolais and in the North, similar to those of Mercurey.

In the Mercurey region the soil in which the vines grow is marly with an amount of limestone (1).

The geological nature of the Côte-d'Or soil and, more specifically, that of the Côte is fairly complex but is composed of three principle elements : limestone, clay and silica. In the areas producing the finest red wines, the percentage of these elements varies at nearly every step. This explains why there are differences in character between growths.

In the well-defined area of fine white wines (from Meursault to Chassagne), one then finds banks of whitish marl which favour this type of wine.

Finally, the vineyards of Chablis are situated on white to light grey soil, coming from white marly limestone rich soil known as Kimmeridge clay.

(1) E. CHANCRIN, *La viticulture moderne.*

Bearing in mind these soil mixes and the lie of the land, one must use fertiliser with care and follow the ways of cultivation.

C) **The Climate**

In order to bring its fruit to maturity, the vine requires a certain amount of heat and luminosity. All the Burgundian vineyards enjoy a Continental type of climate, in other words having cold winters with frequent frosts and hot summers which are occasionally very hot.

But the position of each of the vineyards largely protects the vines from the harsh weather in winter and the freezing conditions of the Spring dawn which are the toughest opponents of the vine. Indeed, by the position (East and South in Beaujolais, Mâconnais and the Mercurey region ; East-South-East in the Côte de Nuits and Beaune ; South-East and South-West in Chablis) and their situation on the hillsides which generally rise to about 600 to 1,500 feet, these vineyards have a better resistance to winter frosts. They are also sheltered from the prevailing westerly winds, making the most of the sun's rays and are reasonably free from humidity.

The general climatic conditions are not the only consideration. Special conditions experienced in years that are too cold, wet or dry, encouraging meteorological accidents, the hatching of parasites, cryptogamic outbreaks or physiological diseases, have also to be considered.

D) **Vinification**

Everything is brought together at the time of vinification. The characteristics and the quality of the able vines, helped by suitable soil and good climate, can either be realised or lost at this point.

It is the vinification (see p. 53) which evaluates all these qualities and is, therefore, a most important part of the combination of events.

Conclusion

To simplify the parts played by these different craftsmen of quality we can show their functions in a brief summary :

— *the vinification* gives birth to a wine accepting all the hazards of this operation ;
— *the vine plant* gives a guarantee of descent ;
— *the soil* shapes the originality of character ;
— *the climate*, if it is favourable, brings the character to perfection, in other words, a great vintage.

But certain unforeseen influences can often perfect or destroy the harmony which exists between these different craftsmen.

In matters concerning wine and its making, things can happen for which there is no obvious reason.

CHAPTER III

THE WINE

The juice that is collected on crushing grapes is called *must*. It possesses certain properties enabling it to be transferred into wine after undergoing a *fermentation*.

Vinification covers the complete process of making wine, "élevage" is to improve and keep the wine, whereas eonology treats wine generally from a scientific point of view.

1. VINIFICATION

A) *The Grape*

The grape is composed of a stalk (acting as a framework and feeding channel) and berries (called "grume" in Burgundy) of which the skin (or pellicule) contains pulp and pips.

The next table shows an average percentage of principle elements which constitute the different parts of the grape (Ferré-Michel analysis) :—

Chemical constitution of a grape	Proportional percentage of a grape			
	Stalk 3-5 %	Skin 10-20 %	Pulp 70-80 %	Pips 2-4 %
Water	42	66	76	30
Cellulose	50	30	0.36	48
Minerals	4.3	1.3	0.07	1.75
(Sulphates, chlorides, phosphates of potassium, calcium and sodium.)				
Sugar (glucose and levulose) ..	—	—	19.5	—
Acids (tartaric, malic and citric).	1.6	0.4	0.6	1
Tannin	1.3	1.5	—	10
Oil	—	—	—	8

B) *The Must*

One obviously finds most of the parts of the grape in the must after pressing. It is therefore very important to know their different functions and chemical properties, also their influence on the future quality of the wine, if one wants to control a vinification correctly.

The *stalk* contains tannin which can impart a certain roughness to the wine (taste of stalk), also water which can alter the amount of alcohol.

As for the *pips*, they are even richer in tannin and if crushed in the must, give the wine a disagreeable astringence. Therefore in certain cases when the quality could be lowered, the stalks are discarded and care taken not to crush the pips.

The *pulp* and *skins* give essential ingredients to the must and wine. The pulp, which is really the juice, contains sugars and acids. It is colourless. But during fermentation the colouring matter in red grape skins (for example from the traditional Burgundy vines — the Pinot and Gamay noir à jus blanc) is dissolved by alcohol and mixed with the must. In addition, the skins are covered with a wax-like coating called "bloom" where yeasts, needed to transform the must into wine, settle along with bacteria which are detrimental to the health of the wine.

C) *Vinification of red wines*

As Dr. Jules Guyot (1) wrote during the last century, *The great art of making good wine is of primitive simplicity. The best results are obtained by the traditional way.*

However, an important development was started in 1938 under the guidance of the late M. Ferré, then Director of the Station Œnologique de Bourgogne at Beaune.

Red grapes are systematically destalked and the long vatting which used to take about twenty days has been replaced by a fast fermentation lasting 4 or 5 days. The wines still keep all their qualities as before but are ready for drinking far sooner.

Modern œnology has given more rational methods to the vinification process and is far better equipped to advise when particular problems arise at the harvest.

(1) *Culture de la vigne et vinification* (Ed. de la Maison rustique).

The Burgundian grower is now conversant with the latest œnological discoveries and makes use of material perfected by the most recent technical developments. He can follow the different phases of the vinification not as a helpless bystander but as a master, being able to put his knowledge to use thus obtaining the results he requires.

Every winemaking business has its own *cuverie* or fermenting room (see opposite). This is where all the material needed for vinification is kept. It is normally situated above or near to *the cellar*, its size depending upon the area of vineyards owned.

It can be equipped with modern equipment (turning vats, automation of the operations, etc.), more or less advanced, according to the investment means of the user and the interest given to the research for an efficient technic favourable to quality.

In the areas of Beaujolais, Mâcon and Chablis, one finds a certain number of *co-operative* cellars but on a much smaller scale compared with those of the South of France. These co-operative cellars are exactly the same as the private ones except that their vatting capacity is greater and more wine can be made at the same time. Their vinification methods are identical.

In the great growth areas, especially on the Côte-d'Or where properties are divided into small plots and where the harvest is small and requires special attention, such large installations are rare and of no consequence. Their only use being to pool the resources of several properties in a village which otherwise would not have sufficient space to cope with the vintage.

✦ ✦ ✦

Just as we have given a general picture of the culture of the vine in setting out a calendar of tasks, we shall now give an appreciation of vinification by studying the various operations in chronological order.

The vinification method described here is very similar to the one used thirty years ago. The œnological and technical advances tend to partially or totally modify this traditional method while, at the same time, trying to respect the fixed constraints to obtain a wine of great quality. These new methods are still exceptions, they involve large investments too expensive for little properties and the interprofession I.N.A.O. has never taken position regarding them.

Crushing and Destemming. — When the grapes arrive at the Fermenting Room they are thrown into a machine called a *stemmer-crusher* which first of all squashes the berries to release the juice (crushing) then throws off the stalks after separating them from the skins and juice (destemming or to be more precise, destalking) (1).

The crushing operation should burst the berries without damaging the pips and stalks. Destemming can be followed by a centrifuge which helps to recover the one to two percent of must sticking to the stalks.

In the Beaujolais region they dispense with crushing so as to obtain a more fruity and tender wine.

Vatting. — The totally or partly crushed grapes are then pumped or carried up by bucket belt into a vat; a large container made of wood (usually oak), cement, plastic, ena-

---

(1) Depending on the year, destalking can be partial or even omitted.

melled steel or even stainless steel, where the various stages of fermentation take place.

The fermentation. — Is the transformation of must into wine. With the action of yeasts the sugar is converted into alcohol and carbon dioxide gas. Physically the fermentation is recognised by a bubbling and a rise in temperature ; physiologically by the multiplication of yeasts and chemically by the appearance of alcohol and colour.

We will not go into the advantages or disadvantages of *open or closed vatting* or vatting with a *floating cap* (the skins collecting on the surface of the liquid, pushed up by the release of carbon dioxide) or the *submerged cap*. Without wishing to generalise too much we shall simply say that in Burgundy they usually use the floating cap method.

During vatting especially at the beginning, pumping over has to be done several times (remixing the must with its cap), to homogenise and aerate the must which stimulates fermentation and eases diffision of colouring matter.

Fermentation calls for careful supervision with frequent checks on temperature and density. A good fermentation should take place around 30 °C. Below 20 °C and above 35 °C yeasts work very slowly and sometimes not at all. It is then necessary to warm up or cool down the must. The cooling process is usually done with special radiators circulating cold water placed in vats. To warm up the must heat exchangers are frequently used. The must circulates inside a double wall tubing system warmed with steam.

As the temperature rises in the vat the density (richness in sugar) lowers proportionally. With the figures read daily from the thermometer and the saccharimeter (for density) two curves can be plotted on a graph so that the fermentation can be followed and regulated as required.

Sulphiting, or addition of sulphur dioxide is now indispensable for all good vinifications. Sulphur dioxide is an antiseptic which, when used correctly, selects the ferments, neutralises bacteria and develops the colouration intensity.

Yeasting has as its main objective, the stimulation and regularisation of the fermentation, by adding specially selected yeasts or carefully chosen native yeasts to the vat. The addition of yeast is not a wide spread practice in Burgundy and when it does occur, native yeasts are used.

De-vatting. — After a fermentation of about four to six days, the wine can be drawn off and separated from the *marc* which mainly consists of skins and pips. De-vatting can be carried out when most of the natural sugar has been transformed into alcohol, that is to say, when the saccharimeter is plunged into the must and reads practically 1,000.

The free run wine (vin de goutte) obtained after de-vatting is pumped into another vat where it will wait to be blended with the *wine from the press (vin de presse).*

Pressing. — Consists of extracting the juice under pressure by using a press.

The press wine collected in this way represents 10-20 % of the free run wine.

In Burgundy, the marc is not usually pressed more than once to avoid too much tannin being introduced into the wine.

The most commonly used presses are the discontinuous vertical screw type, driven by an electric motor. For white wines the tendency is to adopt the horizontal screw press which cuts up the marc automatically.

A new type of pneumatic press has been tried out in Burgundy. It has a large rubber balloon which, when blown up by compressed air, squashes the grapes against the inner surface of a metallic horizontal cage. This type of press is mostly used for the vinification of white wines, it allows for a better extraction with less pressure.

After the free run wine has been blended with the wine from the press, it is transferred into casks where it finishes fermenting.

D) *Vinification of white wines*

The vinification of white wines differs quite considerably from that of red wines. The wine needs no colouring matter so it is unnecessary to leave the skins in contact with the must. Therefore fermentation takes place in cask.

First of all the grapes have to be crushed (free run must) then pressed (press must) without having been de-stalked for the stalks make the pressing easier. Being of a hard nature they form drainage canals thus reducing the springiness of the mass.

A new process for the region which also helps pressing is to pass the crushed grapes through draining chambers or mechanical drainers which collect a certain amount of must and consequently reduces the size of the solid matter to be pressed.

A second pressing is generally carried out after the grapes have been broken up, that is to say, the marc is carefully dug, turned and even crumbled.

The must of these two pressings is added proportionally to the free run must in new oak casks. This gives the wine tannin which is essential for future clarification. They are left unbunged and an ullage of several litres is left so that the froth formed during the fermentation does not overflow. This is a long process taking two to three weeks, working at a low temperature of 15 to 18 degrees centigrade.

Some growers carry out a *débourbage* before fermentation. This means the must is separated from any matter which may be lying in suspension. When the fermentation has finally died down, the casks are rolled at regular intervals to stir up the lees which will reactivate the yeasts converting any remaining sugar into alcohol and clearing the wine.

E) *Vinification of Rosé wines*

In Burgundy this vinification is quite rare, yet it is done occasionally for two reasons :—

a) When "vin rosé" is a speciality of a region ; for instance at Marsannay-la-Côte in the Côte-d'Or ;

b) To prevent the must being too long in contact with the skins on those occasions when the vintage has been spoilt or the grapes are not ripe.

But if the grapes of a great red wine are made into a rosé, the wine loses its appellation. For example a Chambertin would only have the right to be called Bourgogne Rosé.

This rosé vinification from the clear juice of red grapes can be done :

— either like a white wine vinification. It is then called "vinification en gris" (vinification producing a pale red colour). A light pressing, just enough to discharge the required amount of colouring matter for the future wine ;

— or, like a red wine vinification, except the vatting period is very short (several hours).

A rosé wine may never be a blend of red and white wine.

F) *Improvement of the must*

In bad years, a wine may have too few or two many substances which change its normal balance. Therefore, it is important for the grower to know that he can, if necessary, correct the principal faults of the must which may be :—

— deficiency of sugar ;

— deficiency or excess of acidity ;

— deficiency of colour ;

— deficiency of tannin.

Sugaring or *chaptalisation* is the addition of sugar to the must. This is transformed into alcohol during fermentation : 1,700 kg of sugar in 100 litres of must increases the wine by about one degree of alcohol.

In Burgundy, the national and communal regulations authorize chaptalisation under the following restrictions :—

— for white wines and rosé, more than 3.4 kg of sugar for 100 litres of must is prohibited ;

— for red wines more than 3.6 kg of sugar for 100 litres of
   must is prohibited ;
— for all wines more than 250 kg of sugar per hectare is
   prohibited.

This operation cannot be done unless it is supervised
by a representative of the Service des Contributions Indirectes,
who has to be notified three days in advance by a written
declaration.

Acidification and *de-acidification* are rarely undertaken in
Burgundy as they can endanger the quality of the wine.

To intensify the coloration of a wine the harvest can be
heated to extract the colouring matter in the skins. This
technic requires care to avoid the oxydation of the must.

To add tannin to the wines is frequent and advised for
stability during the maturing process. The simplest way of
adding tannin is to ferment the must in new casks. The quantity
of tannin extracted from these casks, even if they have been
previously scalded is usually sufficient.

2. THE CARE
AND TREATMENT OF THE WINE

The care and treatment of the wine start when the fermentation is over and the wine is placed in vats or casks. The
wines of the regional appellations of the Mâconnais and of
Beaujolais are stocked in vats of different capacity. Most of
the great wines, in particular the wines of the Côte-d'Or, are
kept in casks of about 228 litres (see p. 64). The vats are often

stored at ground level but their watertightness and the mass of liquid contained protect the wine against evaporation, oxydation and temperature changes. The casks go down to the cellar below ground level to be kept in the best conditions for the conservation of the barrels and of the wines : neither too damp nor too dry with a constant temperature of 10 to 12 °C.

By tradition the capacities of the casks, different according to the viticultural regions, are as follow:

Name of cask	Capacity in litres		
	Côte-d'Or	Yonne	Beaujolais Mâconnais
Pièce	228	—	215
Demi-pièce or feuillette	114	136	108
Quart or quartaut............	57	—	54

The French word for the care and treatment of wine is called *élevage*. The wine is helped in its development and improvement, be it either physical or chemical. The object is to bring out the qualities of the wine and give it good keeping power.

A) *Care of new wines*

A well made wine (origin, vinification) protected from spoilage (good healthy grapes and clean wine making equipment) needs simple care. It is necessary to clarify and to stabilise the wine to avoid any possible deviations (accidents diseases). The principle procedures are :—

— *topping up* (or *refilling*) : the casks must be constantly filled up to the top (ullage is caused by evaporation or fall in temperature and absorption by the wood). Air pockets can form in which harmful ferment can develop (fleur, acescence) ;

— *rackings,* done to separate the clear wine from the sediment (or lees) which collects at the bottom of the barrel. The first racking after the vinification is called *débourbage* and is generally carried out in the fermenting room;

— *finings,* used to clarify the wine by precipitating the solid particles held in suspension by adding a proteinous substance (albumin, gelatine or casein) or a mineral (bentonite).

B) *Bottling*

When the wine has completely shed its lees and become limpid, sound and free from fermentation it can be bottled. From this point onwards the wine will no longer require watching over and will age naturally.

It is best to filter before bottling. The wine is passed through porous pads which collect the harmful yeast and bacteria and all other matter in suspension. Filtering therefore has a dual role ; it stabilises the wine and makes it perfectly bright.

The tendency in Burgundy is more and more towards bottling wine when young. Indeed, too long a stay in cask tires and dries a wine making it lose quite a lot of its bouquet. In general the great red wines stay two years in cask, whereas

P. POUPON AND P. FORGEOT

3

the great white wines, which should be drunk young, only remain one year. Certain œnologists are experimenting to find out the possibilities of leaving the wine for even shorter periods in the cask.

Red Beaujolais and White Bourgogne Aligoté are the two wines which can be bottled the quickest, as their fruity flavour and youth are their main characteristics. From mid-November, just one month after the vintage, Beaujolais "Nouveau" or "premier" is drunk by many wine lovers and meets with the same success each year.

The bottles used are called "Bourguignonnes". Concerning their origin, it is known that in 1752 a mine was opened to supply the Epinac glassmaking factory which has been built to provide the province with bottles. This factory could produce 1,500 bottles a day (Courtépée, 1847). They contain 75 cl and have long sloping shoulders, short necks, punted bottoms and their normal colour is the green of dead leaves.

There are also half-bottles (37.5 cl) and quarter-bottles (19 cl). The latter being used by aviation companies. A larger capacity is the magnum (double bottle), which is difficult to handle due to its weight and bulkiness.

The wines of Burgundy are intended to be matured for years in the cellar so require well chosen *corks*. These must be supple without being weak, slightly porous, sound and of good size (24 × 48 mm). The cork used generally comes from Portugal and Spain.

Next the bottles are layed down and either stacked on lathes or placed in racks. Stacking with lathes has the advantage of using the minimum of space without any fixtures.

In addition, when the bottles have been removed, the floor is left completely clear (casks could then take their place). But such an operation calls for a certain training and, therefore, is a specialist's job.

This is why stocking on pallets which hold 500 bottles a time are being used more and more.

C) *Ageing in bottle*

Ageing is a natural phenomenon, which explains to a great extent why wine absorbs oxygen from the air while in cask.

But ageing in the bottle, more perceptible in great red wines, still remains a mystery to be solved by œnologists.

A few of them, not knowing how to analyse the subtilty of these slow changes that take place are tempted to age the wine artificially. They have all failed. One cannot age a wine any more than one can rejuvenate a man. It still remains a secret which nature refuses to surrender.

A wine must be kept, writes Roupnel, *for nearly the whole span of a man's life, in the dark subterranean solitude of a cellar, to become great, fulfilling all its promises, tempering its violence, realising its charm, completing its velvety texture and becoming a generous wine whose strength appears tender, who, in its old age will have the purity of an open flower; thanks to a flower that is long dead...*

It is now quite common to compare the life of wine with that of man, for this is the best comparison to understand the respect, delicacy and experience which this "changeable and varying" being has throughout its existence before giving joy and happiness to those who ask for and appreciate its qualities.

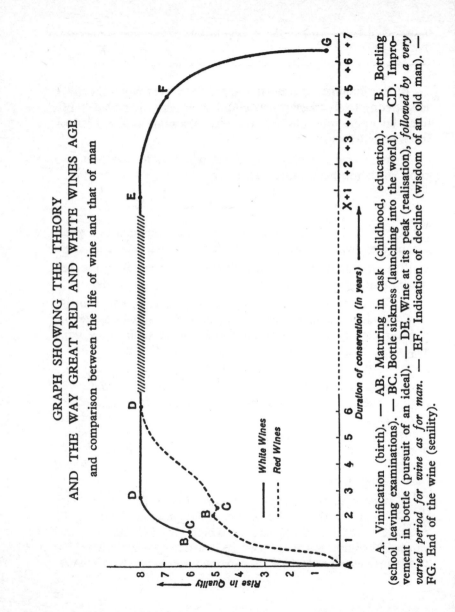

GRAPH SHOWING THE THEORY
AND THE WAY GREAT RED AND WHITE WINES AGE
and comparison between the life of wine and that of man

Duration of conservation (in years)

Rise in Quality

White Wines
Red Wines

A. Vinification (birth). — AB. Maturing in cask (childhood, education). — B. Bottling (school leaving examinations). — BC. Bottle sickness (launching into the world). — CD. Improvement in bottle (pursuit of an ideal). — DE. Wine at its peak (realisation), *followed by a very varied period for wine as for man.* — EF. Indication of decline (wisdom of an old man). — FG. End of the wine (senility).

In our chapter on the vine (p. 53) we have already shown this comparison between man and wine. We shall complete this by a graph and a key (opposite) explaining the theory and the way great red and white wines age.

D) *Non-bacterial disorders and bacterial diseases*

In common with all living beings, wine is not protected against non-bacterial disorders and diseases. In many cases there is a cure by treatment. The best of these and the most sure is prevention. This is done by correct fermentation and well balanced must, followed by care of the wine and its handling in hygienic conditions.

Nevertheless, microbic diseases are always possible and it is necessary to know how to detect them. More often than not, they are characterised by cloudiness and colour change. They are distinguished as follows :—

1. Aerobic diseases (ferments needing air in which to develop) : fleur, acescence ;
2. Anaerobic diseases (ferments not requiring air to develop) : tourne, graisse, amertume, etc. ;
3. Diastatic or chemical diseases : oxidasic casse (brown), ferric casse (blue and white), copper casse.

All these diseases can be treated, but frequently the wine loses some of its quality. All the works devoted to œnology and vinification study these microbial diseases and treatments at some length. We cannot go into the details here.

In addition to these diseases, wine is particularly sensitive to smells and can contract a number of non-bacterial faults which do not actually affect its composition but, even so, give a musty, putrid and rotten taste. (Musty casks or a spoilt vintage). A taste of wood (badly kept casks), tar, petrol, metal, etc. Here again, treatments are rarely efficient and always to the detriment of quality.

E) *Possible changes in bottled wine*

Great wines are a natural and living product. This is why changes can occur during the ageing process and cause cloudiness, deposits and bad tastes.

Certain changes can be seen with the eye. They usually come in the form of cloudiness or a sediment which does not spoil the quality of the wine. It is preferable that the sediment does not reach the consumer's glass and why decanting should be done carefully before serving.

Other changes can only be detected on the nose or palate (taste of cork, mustiness, etc.) They are usually caused by bad storage conditions and can really spoil the quality, up to the point where the wine is undrinkable.

3. ŒNOLOGICAL PRACTICES

In their own interests, growers and merchants usually install a small laboratory near to their fermenting rooms or cellars. Certain simple analyses are indispensable for either controlling the vinification, evaluating a must or wine, ensuring proper care or checking wines prior to purchase. These analyses can be carried out using simple apparatus and little practice. In general, the most useful checks are as follows :—

— *for must :—*

> Determination of sugar, i.e. the future alcoholic content (saccharimeter or refractometer) ;
> Acidity (acidimeter).

— *for wine :—*

> Alcoholic degree (ebulliometer) ;
> Determination of sugar ; total acidity ; volatile acidity ; sulphur ; iron and copper (especially white wines) ;
> Stability in the presence of air (observation of "casses") ;
> Tests before fining ;
> Chromatography on paper (study of the malolactic fermentation).

Most of the big commercial companies have their own laboratories which enable them to make the best selections, to store under the best conditions and to perfect the quality of the wines to be sold.

Analyses of four wines for the year 1978 coming from four Burgundian vines

	BEAUJOLAIS (Gamay)	BEAUNE (Pinot)	MEURSAULT (Chardonnay)	BOURGOGNE ALIGOTÉ (Aligoté)
Density	0,9904	0,9914	0,9911	0,9916
Alcohol..........	12.7°	13.2°	12.6°	11°
Extract	23.2 g	26.8 g	24.8 g	20.9 g
Sugar	< 2 g	< 2 g	< 2 g	< 2 g
Fixed acidity.....	3.50	3.20	4.35	4.40
Volatile acidity ..	0.30	0.45	0.35	0.35

More and more often the winegrowers bottle and commercialize their wines. They call on one of the many private laboratories opened in the last few years who follow the wines of their clients from vinification to bottling.

4. TASTING

But the most important part of analysing a wine is not given by chemical methods. It comes from an organoleptic examination. In other words from tasting.

Tasting is the art of appreciation of the value of a wine, discovering its qualities, detecting its faults and sometimes spotting its origin and its age with the help of the following three human organs : sight, smell and taste. It obviously requires good judgment, but training, coupled with long and frequent practice, is important. A taster cannot improvise anymore than a critic of literature. It requires in one or the other case to have drunk or read everything ; to have assimilated the characters of wine like those of literature ; to have carefully classified them in one's memory and finally be capable of judging them impartially and with authority. The great difficulty for beginners is that no "typical" wine exists that can be used as a standard or starting point. One must, as in art, develop the taste.

The *tasting room* should be well lit and airy, free from smell and heated in winter.

Either a silver (or silver plated) cup or a glass, or both, can be used for tasting. The silver cup or *tastevin* symbolises everything connected with wine in Burgundy. One often takes the tastevin for a curious objet d'art, used as a novel ash-tray, when it is actually a useful piece of equipment. It started to appear at the beginning of the XVIIth century in the hands of wine tasters who, mounted on horseback, went from one cellar to another knowing that their tastevin would not be crushed in the pocket or break if dropped.

The *tastevin* looks like a little silver cup, shallow and fitted with a handle which has often been made into an attractive shape. Its size can vary quite considerably but its shape should remain the same if it is to be of use. The indented facets which give so much charm to a *tastevin* have a functional purpose. They reflect and throw back the light as it crosses the wine so that one can see the colour, limpidity and depth. On the inside of one face, the cupules are so many little mirrors, on the other side the ribbed indentations play with the light. Above, the crown of buttons show the level one must leave between the edge and the surface of the wine. Finally, in the centre the umbilical point is a bulge which reduces the content.

But the *tastevin* which was invented in the age when candles lit the cellars is difficult to use under electric light and the glass has now replaced it.

One can look at the limpidity better in a glass (particularly the tulip type) (1) by placing it in a direct line with the source of light. The bouquet is also easier to appreciate as the glass, closing at the top, directs the scent right to the nose. When

(1) There is now a standard glass (AFNOR NF. V. 09-110) specially made for tasting purposes. It comes in the shape of a lengthened goblet, slightly tapering at the top and having a short stem.

the sight and smell have finished their assessment, a comprehensive appreciation can still not be arrived at until the wine has been tasted. That is to say, after submitting it to the papillae or buds of the tongue. An adequate quantity of wine is held in the mouth, spread over the tongue and rolled over the palate whilst drawing in air into the centre of the mouth. This is done by slowly inhaling and making a gargling noise so dear to tasters. After tasting, the wine is spat out.

To know how to taste intelligently is one of the most precious qualities of a merchant. He must constantly keep a close eye on the state and behaviour of his wine in stock. One could say that he examines it like a doctor. Are the wines developing normally ? Are they ready for bottling ? Are they improving ? Have they reached their peak ? Are they ready for drinking, that is to say, ready for sale ? Are they on the decline ? So many questions to be asked about each of the wines. If one adds to these tastings, the purchases at the vineyards, one can easily see that a merchant is virtually tasting every day of his life.

Like all arts, tasting has its own terminology and below will be found in alphabetical order a few of the expressions currently used in connection with wine :—

AMER : Bitter taste ; reveals itself especially at the end of the tasting, an unpleasant taste often due to an excess of tannin.

APRE : Harsh ; used to describe a rough, hard wine.

ASTRINGENT : Full of tannin.

BOUQUETÉ : A wine which exhales its perfume.

BOURRU : Rough ; refers to a new white wine still on its lees with its fermentation incomplete.

CAPITEUX : Warm and rich in alcohol.

CHARNU : Fat, full, consistant.

CHARPENTÉ : Of good constitution, well made.

COMMUN : Without character, unworthy of a great name.

COMPLET : Complete, having a harmonious blending of characters.

CORSÉ : Robust ; rich in alcohol.

COULANT : Supple, flatters the palate.

COURT : Of feeble flavour and fugitive.

CRU : Too young, green.

DÉPOUILLÉ : Said of a very old wine whose age has robbed it of body and colour.

DISTINGUÉ : Having all the finesse and qualities of its race (see "FIN").

DUR : Hard, a wine with excessive tannin.

ÉQUILIBRÉ : See "COMPLET".

ÉTOFFÉ : Plenty of stuffing.

FIN : Elegant, distinguished, with delicate bouquet.

FRAIS : A wine which has retained the taste of the grape and all the other qualities of a young wine.

FRANC : A wine possessing no underlying taste other than that of the grape.

FRIAND : Fresh, fruity, of agreeable flavour, generally applied to a young wine.

FRUITÉ : Fruity, in the sense of a wine which has retained some of its original grape sugar.

GÉNÉREUX : A wine fairly well-off in alcohol.

GRAS : Rich, which at the same time is fleshy, robust and round.

GOULEYANT : A term generally used for a young Beaujolais which is fresh, light, fruity and pleasant.

LÉGER : A light, pleasing wine with little alcoholic strength and lightly coloured.

MACHE : Said of a wine that fills the mouth, giving the impression of a degree of fullness.

MAIGRE : without fleshiness or fatness, low in alcohol and thin. (the opposite to CORSÉ).

MOELLEUX : Luscious, velvety.

MOU : Flabby, lacking in body, acidity, alcoholic strength and tannin.

NERVEUX : Vigorous, with every promise of improving with age.

PLAT : A flat, dull, wine with no future.

PRIMEUR : A wine which develops certain qualities early and can also be drunk very young.

PUISSANT : Powerful, robust, full of stuffing.

RACÉ : Full of breed, living up to the characteristics of its name.

ROBE : Colour, a wine which enjoys a fine and above all constant colour.

ROND : Full, fleshy, very supple.

SEC : *White wine :* without sugar, typical of the white wines of Burgundy.
  Red   wine : a wine that has lost its softness and bouquet.

SOUPLE : Supple, having neither harshness or astringency.

TERROIR : Earthy. Tang of the soil. When a wine shows drinking qualities peculiar to its locality or breeding.

TUILÉ : Said of an old red wine losing its colour, red-brick or orange-coloured.

USÉ : A wine completely robbed of its vinous qualities caused either by faulty maturing in the barrel or being too long in the bottle.

VELOUTÉ : Very luscious and very supple.

VERT : Young, raw, acid.

VIF : A nervous wine coupled with a certain amount of acidity (opposite to flabby) ; always applies to young wines.

VINEUX : Vinous, high in alcohol, generally lacking finesse.

Chapter IV

THE APPELLATIONS OF ORIGIN IN BURGUNDY

1. THE REGULATIONS

Prior to the xxth century very little legislation was applied to wine.

Satisfaction of the consumer only mattered and the "taste-vin" was the sovereign judge of quality.

It is only as the result of serious crises that the current laws have been promulgated.

At the end of the xixth century the phylloxera crisis caused a wine shortage encouraging abuse and fraud. The law of 1st August 1905 stopped "the deceits and attempted deceits of nature, quality, species, origin and denomination of wine".

After the 1914-18 war the demand for wine increased considerably and was difficult to satisfy. For certain people, sometimes strangers to the profession, it was an opportunity to make money quickly without scruples. This situation gave birth to the law of 6th May 1919 which defined the appellations of origin, stated the rules and enforced their use.

During the crisis and depression of 1930 to 1934 it was realised that the legislation of 1919 whilst solving some of the problems in the viticultural areas, had also permitted additional abuses, especially at the vineyard. It is, therefore, the Decree of 30th July 1935 that now controls the appellations of origin.

The regulation of the controlled appellations of origin is complex and delicate to perfect, all the more because it is evolutionary. The notion of appellation of origin finds its basis in the local fair and constant customs which are not set and which must retain, in their technical evolution, those contributions best for the quality of the product.

Because of the I.N.A.O. each appellation is specified by : the area of production (for surveyed parcels), the authorized varietals, the pruning, the training of the vine, the yield and the minimum and maximum degrees of alcohol.

The maximum yield can be increased and decreased in exceptional years and adjusted to the level of an average harvest for the year under consideration. The vinegrowers can freely claim the appellation of the considered wine within the limits of the annual yield. In the case of excess two cases are taken in consideration by the legislation (decree of October 1974) :—

— if the yield is below the 20 % lower limit (called P.L.C.) of the average annual yield ; in this case the wine could claim its appellation only after an analytical and organoleptical test ;

— or, if the yield is above the 20 % higher limit of the average annual yield. In this case the excess will be compulsorily distilled and the remaining quantity may claim the appellation only after the expert's approval.

These criteria are necessary but not sufficient to guarantee the quality of the wine. This is why since 1974, tasting committees have been created in all the regions of production. These committees examine the wines of the last harvest under the production of the National Institute of Appellations of Origin.

⁎ ⁎ *⁎*

The regulation of the Controlled Appellations of Origin involves severe and minute controls at all stages :—

— *at the property :* control of vine stock, pruning, compulsory declarations of stocks, harvest yields, tasting, etc. ;

— *on leaving the property :* irrespective of the destination, wine may not be moved without either an Excise Sheet (pièce de régie) (1) or a form for receipt (acquit) if it involves a sale to a wholesaler or an exporter ; or a permit (congé or capsule-congé) to show tax has been

(1) The Excise Sheets (receipts or permits) are always printed on green paper for wines of Controlled Appellation and on coarse paper for non-appellation wines. Therefore, outsiders can see at a glance in which category the wine falls.

paid for sales to individuals, grocers, cafés, restaurants, etc. These Excise Sheets are made out by the Administration des Contributions Indirectes and follow the wine the whole length of its journey to final destination.

— *at the wholesalers* : the wine-broker should, on receipt of the wine, register in a special book (the book of Appellations of Origin) the particulars laid out on the "acquit". The same when he resells the wine, he is obliged to accompany the wine with an Excise Sheet (1) for wines in cask and, since 1972, a "capsule-congé" must be used when wine is sold in bottle. In addition, the despatches must be entered in the same Appellation Book, as and when sales are effected.

Stocks are generally checked twice a year by the Service des Contributions Indirectes. The accounts and the wines sold can be checked at any time by the Service de la Répression des Fraudes ;

— *at the retailers* : who must present for inspection the invoices and Excise Sheets covering wines received to all the Services, viz Contributions Indirectes, Appellations d'Origine, Contrôle des Prix, etc. They must, in addition, submit to various formalities in connection with their sales.

(1) However, it should be noted that at the trade level, an invoice permit is often used for sales of wines in case.

2. LABELLING

The label is a real identity card for the wine. It is not only a way to inform the consumer but also to authentigate the product.

The references on the label are subject to regulations by various national laws (the decree of 30th September 1949 in particular) and community regulations (C.E.E., 355/79 and 997/81).

Therefore we show below the principal regulations required for the wines of Controlled Appellation of Origin and table wines, disregarding local wines which are not produced in Burgundy.

A) *Labels intended for Appellation Contrôlée Wines*

Three facts must be shown on the labels and these are compulsory :

— the denomination of the product :

It is the name of the appellation, for example "Bourgogne", with immediatly below the word "Appellation Contrôlée" ;

— the nominal volume of the contents :

It is the quantity of liquid held in the container. It is, most often written in centiliters, but it can also be in milliliters or liters ;

— the name and address of the bottler :

Preceded by the words "blottled by..." the name of the bottler is followed by the address of his principal establishment. If the bottling has been done outside of this establishment it is mentioned. The name of the bottler is complemented, if needed, with his professional activity such as : "vinegrower" or "wine-merchant" when there can be confusion between the name of the commune where he lives and the name of an appellation.

To these compulsory indications it is possible to add some optional informations, we will quote only a few of them :—

— the harvest year :

In France, unlike other countries, the vintage can be mentioned on the bottle only if the totality of the wine contained comes from the same harvest ;

— the place of the bottling :

Information such as "bottled in the region of production" or "bottled in the property" ;

— the name of the varietal :

It would be desirable to add this for the consumer's information ;

— the commercial brand :

Many wine merchants think their wines are worth a special distinction compared to other wines of the same appellation because of the care and treatment given to them. Therefore they create commercial brands to complete the appellation and to give their wines a more personal touch ;

— the country of origin :

This information is compulsory for exportation ;

— some others optional references are : the color of the wine, the mode of elaboration, the names and address of the people belonging to the commercial trade, the official medals awarded to the wine, etc.

B) *Labels intended for Table Wines*

```
                                    75 cl

        La Bonne Tassée
         Vin de Table


       mis en bouteilles par
       F. Dupont   à  F 21200
```

For these wines three references are compulsory :—

— the name of the product such as, in this case, "Table Wine" in visible print ;

— the nominal volume (as with the Appellation Contrôlée wines) ;

— the name and address of the bottler.

To avoid any confusion in the consumer's mind the address of the bottler is a postal code when it can be confused with the name of an Appellation Contrôlée wine.

Most of the optional authorized references for the wines of appellation of origin cannot be used on labels for Table Wine for example the name of the varietal, the vintage, the mode of elaboration, etc. That explains why the professionals use a commercial brand. It is the only way for the consumer to find again a product he enjoyed.

In general, the label of an Appellation Contrôlée wine, Table Wine A.O.V.D.Q.S. or Local Wine should not be designed in such a way as to be misleading. Nor may they include an indication, illustration, picture or symbol which could create confusion in the mind of the buyer regarding the nature, origin, quality or composition of the product or the capacity of the container holding it.

3. THE DIFFERENT CATEGORIES OF A.O.C.

In Burgundy, the large number of appellations causes a complex situation. We have set out the complete list (see page 11).

Before studying them in detail by regions, we will classify them into four main categories :

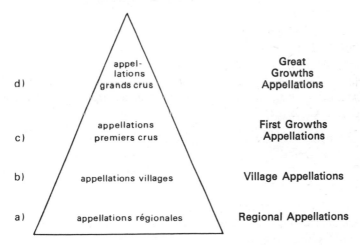

d)	appel-lations grands crus	Great Growths Appellations
c)	appellations premiers crus	First Growths Appellations
b)	appellations villages	Village Appellations
a)	appellations régionales	Regional Appellations

a) *Regional Appellations*

These appellations describe wines which may come from anywhere in the Burgundy area (see p. 95).

b) *Village Appellations*

A large number of Burgundy Villages legally give their name to the wine which has been produced from grapes coming from within their defined area :

Fleurie, Mâcon, etc., in the Beaujolais-Mâconnais ;

Beaune, Volnay, Nuits-Saint-Georges, Meursault, etc., in the Côte-d'Or ;

Chablis in the Yonne.

c) *The first growths appellations*

In each village the vineyards are divided into small parcels or plots known as *climats* in Burgundy. There are several hundreds if not thousands.

The name of these "climats" can be added to the names of the villages so that the exact area where the wine originated can be identified.

In order to recognise the climats which are considered the best, legislation has found a rather too subtle solution which is difficult for the uninitiated to understand. Nevertheless, we will try to explain.

1) The first growths : these are the climats which tradi-tionally are recognised as the best and which are subject to a specific delimitation.

On the labels they can be recognized because they appear :—
— placed after the name of the commune in letters of a size and height which do not exceed those of the appellation ;
— or, printed as above followed by "Premier Cru" ;

— or, replaced by just the words "Premier Cru" (with no control on size of lettering).

Example : For the "climat" of "GRÈVES" in Beaune the label may show :—

— either, BEAUNE GRÈVES ;
— or, BEAUNE GRÈVES Premier Cru ;
— or, BEAUNE PREMIER CRU.

These three presentations must be followed by the words "Appellation Contrôlée".

In the following pages we give a list of names of the "climats" and show the "Premiers crus" or first growths for each appellation, where applicable.

For some years now the list of "Premiers Crus" has been awaiting revision, but the final outcome is still far from being resolved. Therefore, we will give the old list of "Premiers Crus", the only list which is actually valid.

2) The names of lesser known climats can appear on labels but the letter may only be half the height and size of the appellation.

Example : BEAUNE Lulunne.

In this case, the name of the appellation must be placed between the words "Appellation" and "Contrôlée" as in the example below :

BEAUNE Lulunne

Appellation Beaune Contrôlée

d) *The Great Growths*

Finally, among the "climats" a few have enjoyed a high reputation since bygone times. Their name alone is an adequate description and becomes the Appellation : Chambertin, Musigny, Corton, Richebourg, Clos de Vougeot, Montrachet, etc. (in the following pages we identified them with the mention G.C.).

It is most important not to confuse the name "Grand Cru" with that of the village. For example Chambertin and Gevrey-Chambertin, Musigny and Chambolle-Musigny, Corton and Aloxe-Corton, Montrachet and Puligny-Montrachet or Chassagne-Montrachet, etc. The first wine normally being in a superior class to the second.

4. THE RECLASSIFICATION
AND DECLASSIFICATION OF APPELLATIONS

The Producer or the wine merchant may, in most cases, reclassify a wine entitled to an appellation into another of a lower classification.

Therefore, for example, a Chambertin can be reclassified into a Gevrey Chambertin or a Bourgogne.

For each appellation, we will state under the heading "Reclassified" all the descriptions which the wine is legally entitled to claim.

But one must never forget that the reclassification is compulsory when, for any reason, two different appellations have been blended.

The blend of a Beaune and a Pommard, or Chambertin and Clos-Vougeot, etc., can only be sold under the appellation "Bourgogne" ; Mercurey and a Beaujolais Supérieur, under the appellation "Bourgogne Grand Ordinaire", etc.

$$\star^{\star}_{\star}$$

On the other hand, legislation does not allow a controlled appellation wine to be declassified into a non-appellation wine except if the controlled appellation wine is of a lower quality than normal due to technical reasons. In this case, the Répression des Fraudes must be informed and they would decide whether there were adequate reasons to declassify.

CHAPTER V

THE CHARACTERISTICS
OF THE WINES

In the following pages will be discribed all the characteristics of all the Burgundian appellations. Nevertheless it is necessary to specify :—

Average harvest : the harvests fluctuate from year to year because of the hazardous climatic conditions. This explains why we show the average harvest of the vintage 1980 to 1986 inclusive.

Color, type of vine, minimum alcoholic strength : these are the informations give in the decrees of appellations' control.

Maximum yield : this is the basic yield given in the decrees of control. It can be modified according to the year and the climatic conditions (see p. 80). In the following pages it is given in hectoliter per hectare (hl/hectare).

Boundary area : the delimitation of the first growths has not been brought up to date by the experts of the I.N.A.O. since the creation of the appellation of origin. This extensive work is in progress and each time it has been approved by the I.N.A.O. We mentioned the area of the first growths in this heading.

List of the climats classified in first growths : in the same way we mentioned the results of the experts' work from the I.N.A.O. To make the reading easier we did not put the survey numbers of each locality classified in first growths.

1. THE REGIONAL APPELLATIONS

As previously mentioned (p. 87), certain wines are harvested throughout Burgundy. They have the right everywhere to the same appellation.

This explains why certain communes, having a large controlled area, only produce a small quantity of wine under the "village" appellation. No doubt a large quantity of wine is being produced under a regional appellation.

I. — Bourgogne

— colour : red, white and rosé wines (in the case of the last-mentioned the appellation becomes *Bourgogne Clairet* or *Bourgogne Rosé ;*

— types of vines :

For red wines : the Pinot and in the Yonne area, the César and the Tressot. In the Mâcon and Beau-jolais areas the wines made from the "Gamay Noir à jus blanc"—the black Gamay with the white juice—are entitled to the name of Burgundy if produced in the following areas : Brouilly, Chénas, Chiroubles, Côte-de-Brouilly, Fleurie, Juliénas, Morgon, Moulin-à-vent, Saint-Amour ;

For white wines : the Chardonnay and the Pinot Blanc.

— minimum alcoholic strength : red and rosé 10 degrees, white 10.5 degrees ;

— maximum yield : red and rosé, 60 hl/ha ; white, 55 hl/ha ;
— average harvest : white wines, 9,500 hl ; red wines, 101,000 hl ;
— reclassified : Bourgogne Grand Ordinaire.

NOTE :—

a) *Bourgogne Hautes-Côtes de Beaune*
   Bourgogne Hautes-Côtes de Nuits :

   The name of Hautes-Côtes de Beaune or that of Hautes-Côtes de Nuits can be adjoined after approval by a Tasting Commission to that of Bourgogne, Bourgogne Clairet or Bourgogne Rosé for those wines produced within a limited area of various "communes" of Hautes-Côtes de Beaune and Nuits (decree of 4th August 1961).

   — average harvest : Bourgogne Hautes-Côtes de Beaune : white wines, 400 hl ; red wines, 13,700 hl. Bourgogne Hautes-Côtes de Nuits : white wines, 800 hl ; red wines, 8,900 hl.

b) *Bourgogne Irancy*

   The name of Irancy can be adjoined to that of "Bourgogne", "Bourgogne Clairet" or "Bourgogne Rosé", for red wines produced within the limits of the commune of Irancy (Yonne) (decree of the 14th December 1977).

   — average harvest : 2,900 hl.

II. — *a)* Bourgogne Passe Tout Grains

— colour : red or rosé wines ;
— origin : mixture at the time of vinification of two-thirds
  Gamay Noir with the white juice and one-third Pinot ;
— minimum alcoholic strength : 9.5 degrees ;
— maximum yield : 55 hl/hectare ;
— average harvest : 57,100 hl ;
— reclassified : Bourgogne Grand Ordinaire.

b) Bourgogne Aligoté

— colour : white wines only ;
— type of vine : Aligoté (with or without Chardonnay) ;
— minimum alcoholic strength : 9.5 degrees ;
— maximum yield : 60 hl/hectare ;
— average harvest : 45,500 hl ;
— reclassified : Bourgogne Grand Ordinaire.

Bourgogne Aligoté Bouzeron :

> With the decree of the 7th March 1979 the name
> Bouzeron can be adjoined to that of "Bourgogne Ali-
> goté" for the white wines produced exclusively from
> the Aligoté grape and within the limits of the commune
> of Bouzeron (Saône-et-Loire).

— maximum yield : 45 hl/hectare ;
— average harvest : 950 hl.

P. POUPON AND P. FORGEOT   4

III. — Bourgogne Ordinaire
or Bourgogne Grand Ordinaire

— colour : red, white and rosé ;

— types of vine :—

red wines : pinots fins and Gamay Noir à jus blanc ;
In the Yonne : the César and the Tressot ;
white wines : Chardonnay and Pinot Blanc, Aligoté,
Melon de Bourgogne, and in the Yonne, Le Sacy ;

— minimum alcoholic strength : red and rosé 9 degrees,
white 9.5° ;

— maximum yield : red and rosé, 55 hl/hectare white,
60 hl/hectare.

— average harvest : white wines, 2,400 hl ; red wines, 13,300 hl ;

— reclassified : none.

2. THE WINES OF THE YONNE

The Chablis Region

This vineyard, of a relatively modest size, is today confined to about twenty villages around the little town of Chablis and nearly all the wine produced is white. In the past it formed an important viticultural territory situated in Basse-Bourgogne. At that time it spread over four other districts : Tonnerrois, Avallonnais, Joigny and Les Riceys, places which made more red or rosé than white wine. These wines, thanks to the easiness with which they were transported by the rivers Yonne and Seine, were very popular in Paris and Belgium.

Following the phylloxera disaster, the wine growers of Basse-Bourgogne, in face of growing competition from the wines of the South of France, sent their wares to Paris by a new form of transport called the railway. Consequently the Rail Authorities were forced to speed up their expansion but only laid new tracks in the areas capable of producing fine wines. In this way the Cotes de Chablis and its surrounding districts thrived. They were also blessed with mainly limestone soil and sunny slopes on both sides of the little Valley of Serein where the noble Chardonnay vine, which makes first class reliable wine, could be planted.

The Chablis region a "vinous isle" far from the Côte-d'Or is now dedicated to the production of clear, perfumed, lively and light wines. Outside of France, its name has become almost synonymous with "fine dry white wine".

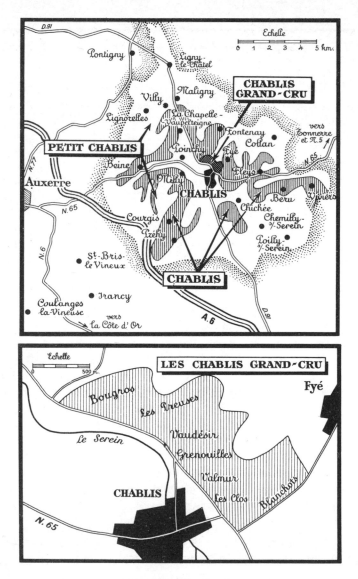

The Chablis Region

In the valley of the Yonne, south of Auxerre, a few villages, such as Irancy and Saint-Bris-le-Vineux produce with unusual vines for Burgundy, agreable wines. These simple appellations are enhanced by their limited quantity.

I. — Chablis Grand Cru

This appellation can equally be followed by the name of a particular "climat" of origin such as : Vaudésir, Preuses, Les Clos, Grenouilles, Bougros, Valmur or Blanchots :—

— colour : white wines only ;
— boundary area : 95 ha ;
— minimum alcoholic strength : 11 degrees ;
— maximum yield : 45 hl/hectare ;
— average harvest : 5,300 hl ;
— reclassified : Chablis Premier Cru, Chablis, Bourgogne or Bourgogne Grand Ordinaire.

II. — Chablis

This appellation may be followed by :—

— either the expression "Premier Cru" or the name of the climat of origin in the case of those wines produced from the plots indicated in the list below ;
— or, just the name of the "climat" in the case of those wines from other plots (see p. 89).

COMMUNE OF CHABLIS

Monts de Milieu, Montée de Tonnerre, Chapelot, Pied-d'Aloue, Côte de Brechain, Vaupoulant, Vaulorent, Vaillons, Châtains, Sécher,

Beugnons, Les Lys, Mélinots, Roncières, Les Épinottes, Montmains, Forêt, Butteaux, Côte de Léchet, Beauroy, Côte de Vaubarousse, Berdiot.

Some of these "Climats" cover other communes.

COMMUNE OF FONTENAY

Côte de Fontenay.

COMMUNE OF MALIGNY

L'Homme-Mort.

COMMUNE OF BEINE

Troesmes, Côte de Savant, Vau Ligneau, Vau de Vey, Vaux Ragons.

COMMUNE OF CHICHÉE

Vaucoupin, Vosgros, Vaugiraut.

COMMUNE OF FLEYS

Les Fourneaux, Morein, Côte des Prés-Girots.

COMMUNE OF COURGIS

Chaume de Talvat, Les Landes et Verjuts, Les Beauregards, Côte de Cuisoy.

— colour : white wines only ;

— boundary area : 1,700 ha (550 ha in first growths) ;

— minimum alcoholic strength : 10 degrees, Premiers Crus : 10.5 degrees ;

— maximum yield : 50 hl/hectare ;

— average harvest : Chablis Premier Cru, 22,000 hl ; Chablis, 38,000 hl ;

— reclassified :—

— *Chablis Premier Cru :* Chablis, Bourgogne or Bourgogne Grand Ordinaire ;

— *Chablis :* Petit Chablis, Bourgogne Grand Ordinaire (but not Bourgogne except if the wine has more than 10.5° and can be clearly specified in order to comply with the necessary controls).

Appreciation : *The wines of Chablis are one of the top ranking white wines of France ; subtly spiritous, plenty of body, finesse, and of fine bouquet ; renowned for their light colour and limpidity. In spite of their long standing popularity their value tends to be higher than their reputation.* (Dr. GUYOT.)

III. — Petit-Chablis

— colour : white wines only ;
— boundary area : 120 ha ;
— minimum alcoholic strength : 9.5 degrees ;
— maximum yield : 50 hl/hectare ;
— average harvest : 6,000 hl ;
— reclassified : Bourgogne Grand Ordinaire (Bourgogne in the same way as Chablis).

IV. — Sauvignon de Saint-Bris (A.O.V.D.Q.S.)

This wine of superior quality (A.O.V.D.Q.S.) was officially recognised by the Ministry of Agriculture in a decree dated the 5th August 1974.

The words "Appellation vin délimité de qualité supérieure" must appear in bold type on labels and the words A.O.V.D.Q.S. should be on the vintage necklet.

— colour : white wine only ;
— boundary area : includes the following communes in the Yonne department : Saint-Bris-le-Vineux, Chitry, Irancy, Vincelottes, Quenne, Saint-Cyr-les-Colons and Cravant, for the last four : 2,834 ha 94 a ;
— type of Vine : only Sauvignon ;
— minimum alcholic strength : 9.5 degrees ;
— maximum yield : 50 hl/hectare ;
— average harvest : 4,000 hl.

3. THE WINES OF THE COTE-D'OR

The Côte-d'Or is the heart of viticultural Burgundy as it contains the essential qualities. The best red and white wines are made in this area and have given Burgundy a universal reputation.

This French province is known throughout the world for its hospitality, its simple and friendly welcome, its good table and good living.

Having already talked about the *Hautes-Côtes de Nuits* and *Hautes-Côtes de Beaune* in the regional appellations (see p. 95), we shall now describe the different appellations of controlled origin which one encounters in the Communes of the *Côte de Nuits* and *Côte de Beaune*. To simplify matters, we shall go from North to South following the Route National 74, which from Dijon borders the vineyards to the east for 30 miles.

A) The Côte de Nuits

The Côte de Nuits starts just to the south of Dijon, at the northern limit of the commune of Fixin, passes through the villages quoted on page 10 and ends at the southern limit of the commune of Corgoloin.

At one time there was a vineyard of choice vines between Dijon and Fixin. It gradually disappeared, nibbled away by town-planning and development. The soil of Marsannay-la-Côte lying in the "Côte de Dijon" is still planted with the Pinot, which makes an excellent Bourgogne rosé (see p. 106).

The Côte de Nuits clearly faces east and is cut into by steep sided valleys. Some 1,500 hectares are found along a line of about 12 miles. The width rarely exceeds 875 yards, and now and then closes to between 220 and 320 yards. The hill tops generally look barren because the out crops of rock prevent the growth of vegetation, except for occasional clumps of grass. It is interesting to note that in certain spots the quarrying of this rock takes the place of the vine. Comblanchien is noted for its quarries, which produce a beautiful marble, but unfortunately interrupt the viticultural landscape.

Commune : MARSANNAY

Controlled appellation (decree of the 19th May 1987) : **Marsannay.**

— colour : red and white wines ;
— minimum alcoholic strength : red wines 10.5 degrees, white wines 11 degrees ;
— maximum yield : red, 40 hl/hectare ; white, 45 hl/hectare ;
— reclassified : Bourgogne or Bourgogne Grand Ordinaire.

Controlled appellation (decree of the 19th May 1987) : **Marsannay Rosé** (new appellation for Bourgogne Rosé de Marsannay).

— colour : rosé ;
— minimum alcoholic strength : 10.5 degrees ;
— maximum yield : 45 hl/hectare ;
— reclassified : Bourgogne or Bourgogne Grand Ordinaire.

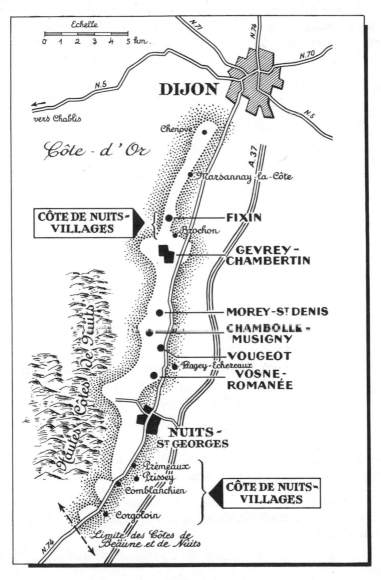

The Côte de Nuits

Commune : FIXIN

Controlled appellation : **Fixin.**

This appellation can be followed :—

—— either by the expression "Premier Cru" or by the name of the "climat" or plot for those wines produced from the plots of land indicated on the list overleaf ;

— or by the actual name of the "climat" for those wines from other plots (see p. 89).

Current list of "climats" classified as "Premier Cru" (first growth).

Les Meix-Bas, Le Clos-du-Chapitre, Aux Cheusots, La Perrière. Les Arvelets, Les Hervelets.

— colour : at the present time red wines only (possibility of white wines) ;

— boundary area : 129 ha 78 a (22 ha 38 in first growths) ;

— minimum alcoholic strength : red wines 10.5 degrees, white 11 degrees, First Growths 11 and 11.5 degrees ;

— maximum yield : white 45 hl/hectare, red 40 hl/hectare ;

— average harvest : 2,500 hl ;

— reclassified : Côte de Nuits-Villages, Bourgogne or Bourgogne Grand Ordinaire.

Appreciation : *These wines are spirituous, of fine colour and a bouquet that develops with age. Tend to be long-lived.* (DANGUY and AUBERTIN.)

Commune : *GEVREY-CHAMBERTIN*

NOTE. — Different decrees have included plots from the commune of Brochon in this commune.

Controlled Appellations :—

I

Chambertin (G.C.) :—

— area : 29 ha 28 a ;
— average harvest : 550 hl.

Chambertin-Clos-de-Bèze (G.C.) (may be named simply "Chambertin") :—

— area : 15 ha 39 a ;
— average harvest : 510 hl.

For these two great growths :—

— colour : red wines only ;
— minimum alcoholic strength : 11.5 degrees.

Appreciation : *It combines grace with vigour ; associating firmness and strength with finesse and delicacy. All these contradictory qualities make an admirable synthesis of unique generosity and complete virtue. The finest that Burgundy can offer.* (Gaston ROUPNEL.)

II

Charmes-Chambertin (or **Mazoyères-Chambertin**) (G.C.) :—

— area : 30 ha 83 a ;
— average harvest : 1,060 hl.

Chapelle-Chambertin (G.C.) :—

— area : 5 ha 48 a ;
— average harvest : 220 hl.

Griotte-Chambertin (G.C.) :—

— boundary area : 2 ha 69 a ;
— average harvest : 57 hl.

Latricières-Chambertin (G.C.) :—

— boundary area : 7 ha 35 a ;
— average harvest : 288 hl.

Mazis-Chambertin (G.C.) :—

— boundary area : 9 ha 10 a ;
— average harvest : 230 hl.

Ruchottes-Chambertin (G.C.) :—

— boundary area : 3 ha 30 a ;
— average harvest : 106 hl.

For all these wines :—

— colour : red wines only ;
— minimum alcoholic strength : 11.5 degrees ;
— maximum yield : 37 hl/hectare ;
— reclassified : Gevrey-Chambertin (First Growth or otherwise), Bourgogne or Bourgogne Grand Ordinaire.

Appreciation : *Chapelle, Griotte and Charmes have the right like Les Ruchottes, Les Mazis, les Latricières, to the appella-*

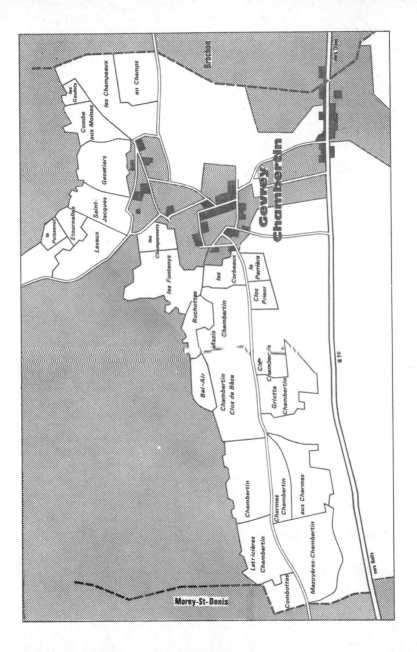

tion "*Chambertin*" to be added to their proper name. And nothing
is more correct than this old usage. Between Chambertin on the one
hand and Latricières and Charmes on the other there is an appreciable difference in vigour and robustness which, in good years, is
compensated by finesse; that is to say, more perceptible and
refined. (Gaston ROUPNEL.)

III

Gevrey-Chambertin

This appellation can be followed by :—

— either the expression "Premier Cru" or the name of the
  "climat" of origin for those wines produced in the plots
  indicated in the list below ;
— or, just the name of the "climat" in the case of those wines
  from other plots (see p. 89).

Current list of classified "First Growth" climats :—

CLOS DES VÉROILLES, LE CLOS SAINT-JACQUES

Aux Combottes, Bel-Air, Cazetiers, Combe-aux-Moines, Estour-
nelles, Lavaut, Poissenot, Champeaux, Les Goulots, Issarts, Les
Corbeaux, Cherbaudes, La Perrière, Clos-Prieur, Le Fontenay, Cham-
ponnets, Au Closeau, Craipillot, Petite-Chapelle, Clos-du-Chapitre.

— colour : red wines only ;
— boundary area : 445 ha 41 a (85 ha 53 a in First Growths) ;
— minimum alcoholic strength : 10.5 degrees. First
  Growths 11 ;
— maximum yield : 40 hl/hectare ;

— average harvest : 15,000 hl ;
— reclassified : Bourgogne or Bourgogne Grand Ordinaire.

Appreciation : *Firm, powerful and well coloured wines, full of flesh coupled with an agreeable "nose".* (Gaston ROUPNEL.)

Commune : *MOREY-SAINT-DENIS*

Controlled Appellations :—

I

Bonnes-Mares (G.C.) :—
— boundary area : 15 ha 06 a (the other part in Chambolle-Musigny has 13 ha 54 a) ;
average harvest : 412 hl.

Clos-des-Lambrays (G.C.) :—
— boundary area : 8 ha 74 a ;

Clos-Saint-Denis (G.C.) :—
— boundary area : 6 ha 63 a ;
— average harvest : 191 hl.

Clos-de-la-Roche (G.C.) :—
— boundary area : 16 ha 90 a ;
— average harvest : 556 hl.

Clos-de-Tart (G.C.) :—
— boundary area : 7 ha 53 a ;
— average yield : 224 hl.

For these four wines :

— colour : red wines only ;
— minimum alcoholic strength : 11.5 degrees ;
— maximum yield : 35 hl/hectare ;
— reclassified : Morey-Saint-Denis (whether First Growth or not) ; Bourgogne or Bourgogne Grand Ordinaire.

Bonnes-Mares can be declassified in "Chambolle-Musigny" (whether First Growth or not) if the wine come from this commune.

Appreciation : *The great wines of Morey are powerful nectars ; plenty of stuffing, full of vitality and bouquet with a somewhat pronounced perfume of strawberries or violets.* (Dr. RAMAIN.)

II

Morey-Saint-Denis

This appellation can be followed by :—

— either the expression "Premier Cru" or the name of the "climat" of origin for those wines produced in the plots indicated in the list below ;
— or just the name of the "climat" in the case of those wines from other plots (see p. 89).

Current list of classified "First Growth" climats :—

Les Ruchots, Les Sorbés, Le Clos-Sorbés, Les Millandes, Le Clos-des-Ormes, Monts-Luisants, La Bussière, Aux Charmes, Les Char-

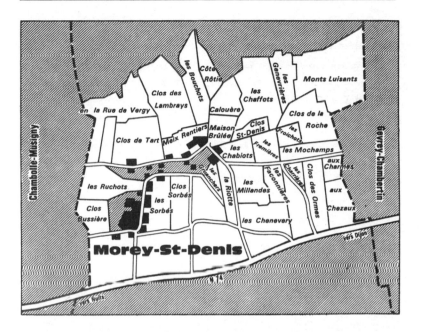

rières, Côte-Rôtie, Les Genevrières, Les Chaffots, Les Chénevery, La Riotte, Le Clos-Baulet, Les Gruenchers, Les Façonnières, Les Blanchards, Aux Cheseaux, Le Village.

— colour : nearly all red wines ;
— total area : 108 ha 32 a (27 ha 75 a in First Growths) ;
— minimum alcoholic strength : reds 10.5 degrees, whites 11, First Growths 11 and 11.5 degrees respectively ;
— maximum yield : red, 40 hl/hectare ; white, 45 hl/hectare ;

— 115 —

— average harvest : white wines, 40 hl; red wines, 2,800 hl;
— reclassified : Bourgogne or Bourgogne Grand Ordinaire.

Appreciation : *A fine colour, a bouquet which develops with age, plenty of body, vinosity, and tends to be long-lived.* (DANGUY and AUBERTIN.)

Commune : CHAMBOLLE-MUSIGNY

Controlled Appellations :—

I

Musigny (G.C.) :—

— colour : almost entirely red wines (a little white Musigny);
— boundary area : 10 ha 70 a ;
— minimum alcoholic strength : reds 11.5, whites 12 degrees ;
— maximum yield : red, 35 hl/hectare; white, 40 hl/hectare ;
— average harvest : 260 hl of red and 10 hl of white;
— reclassified : Chambolle-Musigny (First Growth or otherwise), Bourgogne or Bourgogne Grand Ordinaire for the red wines, Bourgogne or Bourgogne Grand Ordinaire for the white wines.

Appreciation : *The Musigny, the wine of silk and lace; wherein its supreme delicacy ignores all violence and can conceal its strength.* (Gaston ROUPNEL.)

Bonnes-Mares (G.C.) :—

— area : 13 ha 54 a (the remaining part is in Morey-Saint-Denis), see that commune.

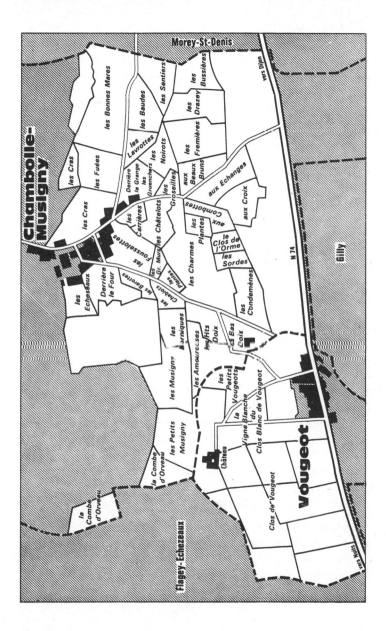

II

Chambolle-Musigny

This appellation can be followed by :—

— either the expression "Premier Cru" or the name of the "climat" of origin for those wines produced in the plots indicated in the list below ;
— or, just the name of the "climat" in the case of those wines from other plots (see p. 89).

Current list of classified "First Growth" climats (for totality or part) :—

LES AMOUREUSES, LES CHARMES

Les Gras, Les Borniques, Les Baudes, Les Plantes, Les Hauts-Doix, Les Chatelots, Les Gruenchers, Les Groseilles, Les Fuées, Les Lavrottes, Derrière-la-Grange, Les Noirots, Les Sentiers, Les Fousselottes, Aux Beaux-Bruns, Les Combottes, Aux Combottes, Aux Echanges, Les Carrières, Les Chabiots, La Combe d'Orveau.

— colour : red wines only ;
— total area : 169 ha 46 a (60 ha 90 a in First Growths) ;
— minimum alcoholic strength : 10.5 degrees. First Growths 11° ;
— maximum yield : 40 hl/hectare.
— average harvest : 4,800 hl ;
— reclassified : Bourgogne or Bourgogne Grand Ordinaire.

Appréciation : *Of high vinosity, fine colour and rich in ether. They have a fine bouquet and many wine experts are of the opinion that these wines are the most scented, fine and delicate of the whole of the Côte de Nuits.* (DANGUY and AUBERTIN.)

Commune : *VOUGEOT*

Controlled Appellations :—

I. — **Clos-de-Vougeot** (G.C.)

— colour : red wines only ;
— boundary area : 50 ha 97 a ;
— minimum alcoholic strength : 11.5 degrees ;
— maximum authorised yield : 35 hl/hectare ;
— average harvest : 1,500 hl ;
— reclassified : Vougeot (whether First Growth or otherwise), Bourgogne or Bourgogne Grand Ordinaire.

Appreciation : *Clos-de-Vougeot, along with Romanée, Chambertin and a few others, ranks first not only amongst the wines of the Côte d'Or but possibly even the whole of France.* (Dr. MORELOT.)

II. — **Vougeot**

This appellation can be followed by :—

— either the expression "Premier Cru" or the name of the "climat" of origin in the case of wines from parcels indicated in the list below ;
— or just the name of the "climat" for wines coming from other plots (see p. 89).

Current list of classified "First Growth" :—

Le Clos-Blanc, Les Petits-Vougeots, Les Cras, Clos-de-la-Perrière.

— colour : red and white wines ;
— boundary area : 16 ha 50 a (11 ha 68 a in First Growths);
— minimum alcoholic strength : reds 10.5, whites 11, First
    Growths 11 and 11.5 degrees respectively ;
— maximum yield : red, 40 hl/hectare ; white 45 hl/hectare ;
— average harvest : white wines, 45 hl ; red wines, 450 hl ;
— reclassified : Bourgogne or Bourgogne Grand Ordinaire.

Commune : *VOSNE-ROMANÉE*

NOTE. — Different decrees have included certain plots in this Commune which, in fact, are in the Commune of Flagey-Échézeaux.

Controlled Appellations :—

I

Romanée-Conti (G.C.) :—

— area : 1 ha 81 a ;
— average harvest : La Romanée-Conti was one of the last
    vineyards to conserve the ungrafted French root stock.
    The lack of carbon sulphide during the last war led
    to its destruction by phylloxera. It was replanted with
    grafted stock and the first wine was made in 1952.
    Average harvest : 40 hl.

Appreciation : *A magnificent wine having a penetrating bouquet of violets mixed with cherries. A colour of sparkling rubies and a finesse to please any palate.* (Dr. RAMAIN.)

Richebourg (G.C.) :—

— boundary area : 8 ha 03 a ;
— average harvest : 200 hl.

Appreciation : *This splendid growth which possesses an incomparable velvety and rich bouquet is one of the most sumptuous wines of Burgundy.* (Camille RODIER.)

Romanée (G.C.) :—

— boundary area : 0 ha 85 a ;
— average harvest : 30 hl.

La Tâche (G.C.) :—

— boundary area : 6 ha 06 a ;
— average harvest : 135 hl.

Romanée-Saint-Vivant (G.C.) :—

— boundary area : 9 ha 44 a ;
— average harvest : 200 hl.

Grands-Échézeaux (G.C.) :—

— boundary area : 9 ha 14 a ;
— average harvest : 250 hl.

Échézeaux (G.C.) :—

— boundary area : 36 ha 10 a ;
— average harvest : 1,050 hl.

For the above-mentioned seven Growths :—

— colour : red wines only ;
— minimum alcoholic strength : 11.5 degrees ;
— maximum yield : 35 hl/hectare ;
— reclassified : Vosne-Romanée (whether First Growth or not), Bourgogne or Bourgogne Grand Ordinaire.

II. — **Vosne-Romanée**

This appellation may be followed by :—

— either the expression "Premier Cru" or the name of the "climat" for wines coming from the plots indicated on the list below ;
— or, just the name of the "climat" for wines coming from other plots (see p. 89).

Current list of classified "First Growth" climats :—

Aux Malconsorts, Les Beaux-Monts, Les Suchots, La Grand'Rue, Les Gaudichots, Aux Brûlées, Les Chaumes, Aux Reignots, Le Clos-des Réas, Les Petits-Monts.

— colour : red wines only ;
— total area : 161 ha 77 a (58 ha 04 a in First Growths), Flagey-Échézeaux included ;
— minimum alcoholic strength : 10.5 degrees. First Growths 11 ;
— maximum yield : 40 hl/hectare ;
— average harvest : 5,300 hl ;
— reclassified : Bourgogne or Bourgogne Grand Ordinaire.

Appreciation : *No ordinary wines are to be found in Vosne.* (COURTÉPÉE.)

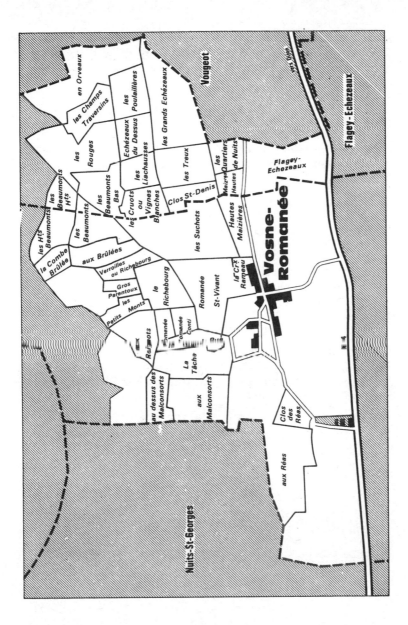

Commune : *NUITS-SAINT-GEORGES*

NOTE. — Decrees have included in this Commune certain vineyard plots which are actually situated in the Commune of Premeaux.

Controled Appellation : **Nuits or Nuits-Saint-Georges.**

This appellation may be followed by :—

— either the expression "Premier Cru" or the name of the "climat" of origin in the case of those wines produced from the plots indicated in the list below ;

— or, just the name of the "climat" in the case of those wines from other plots (see p. 89).

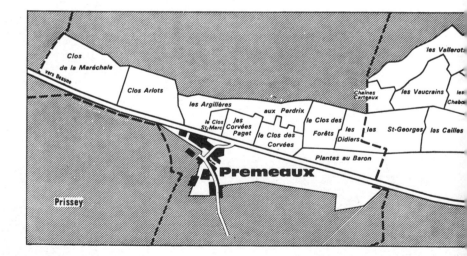

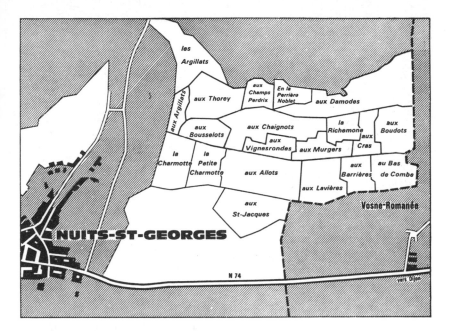

les
Argillats

aux Thorey

aux
Champs
Perdrix

En la
Perrière
Noblet

aux Damodes

aux
Argillats

aux
Bousselots

aux Chaignots

la
Richemone

aux
Cras

aux
Boudots

aux
Vignesrondes

aux Murgers

la
Charmotte

la
Petite
Charmotte

aux Allots

aux
Barrières

au Bas
de Combe

aux Lavières

aux
St-Jacques

Vosne-Romanée

NUITS-ST-GEORGES

N 74

vers Dijon

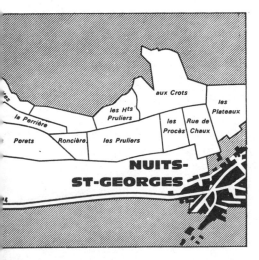

aux Crots

les Hts
Pruliers

les
Plateaux

le Perrière

les
Procès

Rue de
Chaux

Porets

Roncière

les Pruliers

NUITS-
ST-GEORGES

74

Current list of classified "First Growth" or Premier Cru climats :—

LES SAINT-GEORGES, LES VAUCRAINS, LES CAILLES

AT NUITS : Les Porets, Les Pruliers, Les Hauts-Pruliers, Aux Murgers, La Richemone, Les Chabœufs, Les Perrières, Roncière, Le Procès, Rue-de-Chaux, Aux Boudots, Aux Cras, Aux Chaignots, Aux Thorey, Aux Vignes-Rondes, Aux Bousselots, Les Poulettes, Les Crots, Les Vallerots, Aux Champs-Perdrix, Perrière-Noblet, Les Damodes, Les Argillats, En La Chaîne-Carteau, Château-Gris.

AT PREMEAUX : Clos-de-la-Maréchale, Clos-Arlots, Clos-des-Argillières, Clos-des-Grandes-Vignes, Clos-des-Corvées, Les Didiers, Aux Perdrix, Les Corvées-Paget, Le Clos-Saint-Marc, Clos des Forêts-Saint-Georges, Les Terres-Blanches, Les Argillières.

— colour : almost entirely red wines ;
— total area : 318 ha 11 a (142 ha 78 a in First Growths) ;
— minimum alcoholic strength : red wines 10.5, whites 11, "First Growths" 11 degrees for red wines and 11.5 for white ;
— maximum yield : red, 40 hl/hectare ; white, 45 hl/hectare ;
— average harvest : white wines, 20 hl ; red wines, 10,500 hl ;
— reclassified : Bourgogne or Bourgogne Grand Ordinaire.

Appreciation : *Generally speaking the wines of Nuits have less firmness and harshness than those of Gevrey and mature more rapidly ; they have more body and colour than those of Chambolle-Musigny.* (Dr. LAVALLE.)

Appellation : **Côte de Nuits-Villages.**

Various Communes of the Côte de Nuits sell a part of their wine under this appellation ; this right has to be claimed at the declaration of the harvest. These communes are : —

FIXIN	115 ha 78 a
BROCHON	41 – 58 –
PRISSEY	11 – 99 –
COMBLANCHIEN	55 – 27 –
CORGOLOIN	81 – 08 –
TOTAL AREA..........	305 ha 70 a

— colour : Almost entirely, red wine ;
— minimum alcoholic strength : 10.5 degrees for red and 11 for white ;
— maximum yield : red, 40 hl/hectare ; white, 45 hl/hectare ;
— average harvest : white wines, 12 hl ; red wines, 6,500 hl ;
— reclassified : Bourgogne or Bourgogne Grand Ordinaire (never in Nuits).

IMPORTANT NOTE. — Wines coming from other Communes of the Côte de Nuits (Nuits, Gevrey-Chambertin, etc.) can never be sold under the appellation "Côtes-de-Nuits-Villages".

B) The Côte de Beaune

The Côte de Beaune starts at the Northern limit of the commune of Ladoix-Serrigny and finishes in the Saône-et-Loire, after passing through the villages mentioned on page 19. It is wider and longer than the Côte de Nuits by several miles, and has more land under vines, about 3,000 ha in total, which is nearly twice the size of the Côte de Nuits.

Here the vine covered hillsides generally face east but when numerous valleys penetrate the hillsides, they tend to face the South East and take shelter from the North wind and frost. The scenery is less harsh than that of the Côte de Nuits. These hills are generally rounded and have well balanced even slopes. The climbing vines grow uninhibited almost right up to the summits which are covered with boxtrees and junipers.

The Côte de Meursault, scarred by old quarries rises up from the middle of the Côte de Beaune, 6 miles south of Beaune, between the R.D. 973 which goes to Autun and the R.N. 6 leading to Paris. It deserves to be mentioned separately as it is the only hill in the Côte-d'Or where the soil is perfectly suited to the chardonnay vine which produces fine white wines. Meursault, Puligny-Montrachet and Chassagne-Montrachet are the three communes on this Côte.

Commune : LADOIX-SERRIGNY

Controlled Appellations :—

I

Corton (G.C.) (see Aloxe-Corton).
Corton-Charlemagne (G.C.) (see Aloxe-Corton).

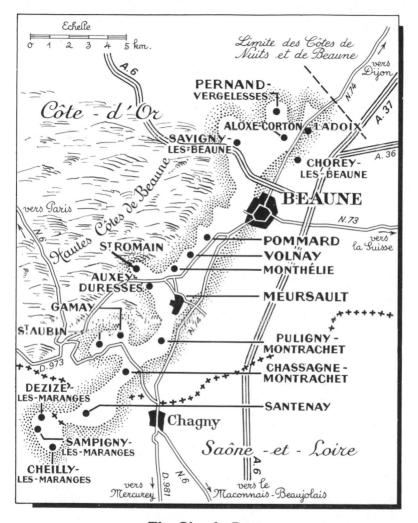

The Côte de Beaune

P. POUPON AND P. FORGEOT

II

Ladoix :—

This appellation may be followed by :—

— either the expression "Premier Cru" or the name of the climat of origin in the case of wines from parcels indicated in the list below ;

— or just the name of the "climat" for wines coming from other plots (see p. 89).

Current list of classified "First Growths" climats :—

La Miraude, La Corvée, Le Clou-d'Orge, Les Joyeuses, Bois-Roussot, Basses-Mourottes, Hautes-Mourottes.

— colour : red and white wines ;

— area : 135 ha 03 a ;

— minimum alcoholic strength : reds 10.5, whites 11 degrees ;

— maximum yield : red, 35 hl/hectare ; white, 40 hl/hectare ;

— average harvest : white wines, 90 hl ; red wines, 1,800 hl ;

— reclassified : red see p. 164 ; white : Bourgogne or Bourgogne Grand Ordinaire.

Commune : ALOXE-CORTON

NOTE. — Decrees have included certain plots situated in the territory of the Communes of Ladoix-Serrigny and Pernand-Vergelesses.

Controlled Appellations :—

I

Corton (1) (2) (G.C.) :—

— boundary area : 160 ha 19 a ;
— colour : red and white wines ;
— average harvest : white wines, 50 hl ; red wines, 2,900 hl.

Corton-Charlemagne (2) (G.C.) :—

— boundary area : 71 ha 88 a ;
— colour : white wines only ;
— average harvest : 1,300 hl.

Charlemagne (2) (G.C.) :—

— boundary area : 62 ha 94 a ;
— colour : white wines only ;
— average harvest : for some years now no declaration of annual output has been made under this name.

For these three wines :—

— minimum alcoholic strength : reds 11.5 and whites 12 degrees ;
— maximum yield : red, 35 hl/hectare ; white, 40 hl/hectare ;
— reclassified : Aloxe-Corton (whether First Growth or not), Bourgogne or Bourgogne Grand Ordinaire.

(1) Note that Corton is sometimes followed by the name of the plot where the wines come from : Clos-du Roi, Renardes, Bressandes, Pougets, Perrières, Languettes, La Vigne-au-Saint, etc.
(2) Some parcels may claim, depending on the producter's choice, one of these three appellations, especially for 17 ha 26 a in Pernand-Vergelesses.

Appreciation : *The wines of Corton in a good year are perfect ; worthy of offering to the most discriminating gourmets, to be served on the most august occasions.* (Dr. LAVALLE.)

Corton-Charlemagne : "A seductive wine high in alcohol content, golden in colour and spreading in the mouth. It has a perfume of cinnamon and a hint of gun flint in its taste". (Camille RODIER.)

II

Aloxe-Corton

This appellation may be followed by :—

— either the expression "Premier Cru" or the name of the "climat" of origin in the case of those wines produced from the plots indicated in the list below ;
— or, just the name of the "climat" for those wines from other plots (see p. 89).

Current list of classified "First Growth" climats :—

COMMUNE OF LADOIX-SERRIGNY

La Maréchaude, La Toppe-au-Vert, La Coutière, Les Grandes-Lolières, Les Petites-Lolières, Basses-Mourettes.

COMMUNE OF ALOXE-CORTON

Les Valozières, Les Chaillots, Les Meix, Les Fournières, Les Maréchaudes, En Pauland, Les Vercots, Les Guérets.

— colour : nearly all red wine, a little white (1 %) ;
— boundary area : 127 ha 30 a (37 ha 59 a in first growths) ;

— minimum alcoholic strength : reds 10.5, whites 11, First
   Growths reds 11 degrees, whites 11°5 ;
— maximum authorised yield : red, 40 hl/hectare ; white,
   45 hl/hectare ;
— average harvest : white wines, 20 hl ; red wines, 4,700 hl ;
— reclassified : Bourgogne or Bourgogne Grand Ordinaire.

Appreciation : *These are the firmest, and the most frank
wines of the entire Côte de Beaune.* (Dr. LAVALLE.)

Commune : *PERNAND-VERGELESSES*

Controlled Appellations :—

I

Corton (G.C.) (see Aloxe-Corton) ;
Corton-Charlemagne (G.C.) (see Aloxe-Corton) ;
Charlemagne (G.C.) (see Aloxe-Corton).

II

Pernand-Vergelesses

This appellation may be followed by :

— either the expression "Premier Cru" or the name of the
   "climat" of origin in the case of those wines produced
   from the plots indicated in the list below ;

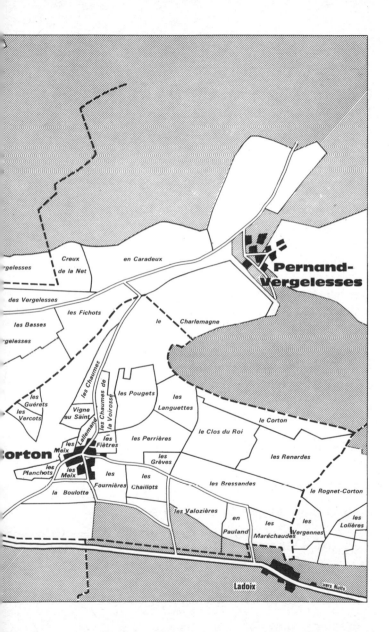

— or, just the name of the "climat" in the case of those wines from other plots (see p. 89).

Current list of classified "First Growth" climats :—

ILE-DES-VERGELESSES

Vergelesses, Creux-de-la-Net, Les Fichots, En Caradeux.

— total area : 194 ha 14 a (56 ha 51 a in first growths);
— colour : red and white wines ;
— minimum alcoholic strength : reds 10.5, whites 11, First Growths reds 11 degrees, whites 11.5 ;
— maximum yield : red, 40 hl/hectare ; white, 45 hl/hectare ;
— average harvest : white wines, 600 hl ; red wines, 2,900 hl ;
— reclassified : red (see p. 164) ; white : Bourgogne or Bourgogne Grand Ordinaire.

Appreciation : *These wines are inclined to be slightly firmer than those of Savigny ; plenty of strength and they keep well.* (DANGUY and AUBERTIN.)

Commune : SAVIGNY-LÈS-BEAUNE

Controlled appellation : **Savigny.**

This appellation may be followed by :—

— either the expression "Premier Cru" or the name of the "climat" of origin in the case of those wines produced from the plots indicated in the list below ;

— or, just the name of the "climat" in the case of those wines from other plots (see p. 89).

Current list of classified "First Growth" climats (for totality or part) :—

AUX VERGELESSES, BATAILLIÈRE
LES MARCONNETS, LA DOMINODE, LES LAVIÈRES

Basses-Vergelesses, Aux Gravains, Les Peuillets, Aux Guettes, Les Talmettes, Les Charnières, Aux Fourneaux, Aux Clous, Aux Serpentières, Les Narbantons, Les Hauts-Marconnets, Les Hauts-Jarrons, Redresculs, Les Rouvrettes, Petits-Godeaux, Champ-Gevrey, Les Jarrons.

— colour : principally red wines but some white wines ;
— boundary area : 375 ha 35 a (141 ha 30 a in first growths) ;
— minimum alcoholic strength : reds 10.5 degrees, whites 11, First Growths red 11 degrees, white 11.5 ;
— maximum yield : red, 40 hl/hectare ; white, 45 hl/hectare ;
— average harvest : white wines, 400 hl ; red wines, 11,100 hl ;
— reclassified : red (see p. 164) ; white : Bourgogne or Bourgogne Grand Ordinaire.

Appreciation : *These scented, soft and fresh wines are not only rich in bouquet but also good for the health.* (Camille RODIER.)

Commune : *CHOREY-LÈS-BEAUNE*

Controlled Appellation : **Chorey-lès-Beaune.**
— colour : red and white wines ;
— total area : 137 ha 72 a (no first growths) ;

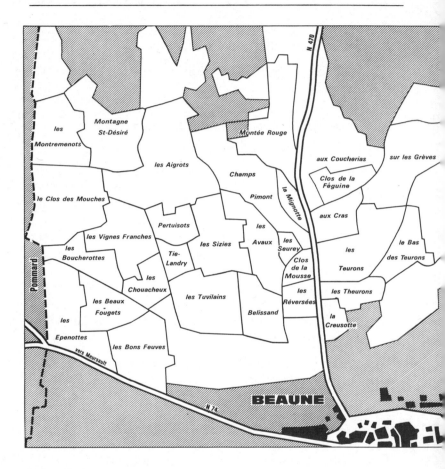

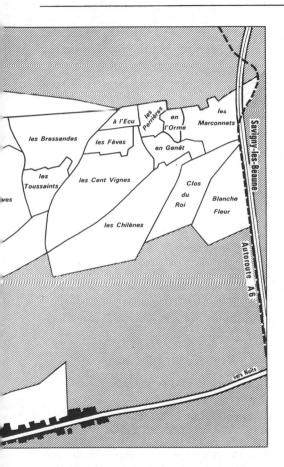

— minimum strength : reds 10.5 and whites 11 degrees ;
— maximum yield : red, 40 hl/hectare; white, 45 hl/hectare ;
— average harvest : red wines, 5,300 hl ; white wines, 15 hl ;
— reclassified : red (see p. 164) ; white : Bourgogne or Bourgogne Grand Ordinaire.

Commune : BEAUNE

Controlled Appellations :—

I. — **Beaune**

This appellation may be followed by :—

— either the expression "Premier Cru" or the name of the "climat" of origin in the case of those wines produced from the plots indicated in the list below ;
— or, just the name of the "climat" in the case of those wines from other plots (see p. 89).

Current list of classified "First Growth" climats :—

LES MARCONNETS, LES FÈVES, LES BRESSANDES
LES GRÈVES, LES TEURONS

Le Clos-des-Mouches, Champs-Pimont, Clos-du-Roi, Aux Coucherias, En l'Orme, En Genêt, Les Perrières, A l'Écu, Les Cent-Vignes, Les Toussaints, Sur-les-Grèves, Aux Cras, Le Clos-de-la-Mousse, Les Chouacheux, Les Boucherottes, Les Vignes-Franches, Les Aigrots, Pertuisots, Clos-Saint-Landry, Les Sisies, Les Avaux, Les Reversées, Le Bas-des-Teurons, Les Seurey, La Mignotte, Montée-Rouge, Les Montrevenots, Les Épenottes, Les Tuvilains, Belissand, Clos-des-Avaux, Clos-des-Ursules, Clos-de-l'Écu.

— colour : principally red wines, but some white wines ;
— boundary area : 451 ha 86 a (320 ha 01 a in first growths) ;
— minimum alcoholic strength : reds 10.5, whites 11, First
    Growths red 11 degrees, wines white 11.5 ;
— maximum yield : red, 40 hl/hectare ; white, 45 hl/hectare ;
— average harvest : white wines, 450 hl ; red wines, 12,800 hl ;
— reclassified : Côte de Beaune, Bourgogne or Bourgogne
    Grand Ordinaire.

Appreciation : *I consider that the famous wines of Beaune
are worthy of the highest praise. In good years the "Best Cuvées"
can only be detected from the other fine wines by the most experienced and are sold at a very high price. Even the "Secondes
Cuvées" are princely being ideal partners for roasts at the family
table.* (Dr. LAVALLE.)

II. — Côte de Beaune

— colour : red and white wines ;
— boundary area : that of "Beaune" plus 51 ha 97 a ;
— minimum alcoholic strength : red 10.5 degrees, white 11° ;
— maximum yield : red, 40 hl/hectare ; white, 45 hl/hectare ;
— average harvest : red wines, 1,000 hl ; white wines, 140 hl ;
— reclassified : see page 164.

NOTE. — This appellation must not be confused with
"Côte de Beaune-Villages" which is an entirely different
appellation.

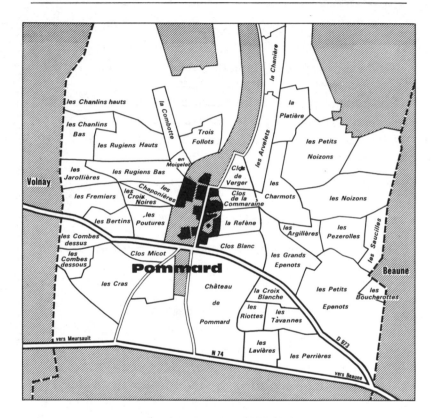

Commune : POMMARD

Controlled Appellation : **Pommard.**

This appellation may be followed by :—
— either the expression "Premier Cru" or the name of the

"climat" of origin in the case of those wines produced from the plots indicated in the list below ;
— or, just the name of the "climat" in the case of those wines from other plots (see p. 89).

Current list of classified "First Growth" climats :—

LES RUGIENS-BAS, LES RUGIENS-HAUTS, LES GRANDS-ÉPENOTS

Les Petits-Épenots, Clos-de-la-Commaraine, Clos-Blanc, Les Arvelets, Les Charmots, Les Argillières, Les Pézerolles, Les Boucherottes, Les Saussilles, Les Croix-Noires, Les Chaponnières, Les Fremiers, Les Bertins, Les Jarollières, Les Poutures, Le Clos-Micot, La Refène, Clos-du-Verger, Derrière-Saint-Jean, La Platière, Les Chanlins-Bas, Les Combes-Dessus, La Chanière, Village.

— colour : red wines only ;
— total area : 336 ha 82 a (125 ha 19 a in first growths) ;
— maximum yield : 40 hl/hectare ;
— minimum alcoholic strength : 10.5 degrees. First Growths 11° ;
— average harvest : 9,600 hl ;
— reclassified : Bourgogne or Bourgogne Grand Ordinaire.

Appreciation : *Strong wines, well coloured, full of frankness and good keeping qualities.* (Dr. MORELOT.)

Commune : VOLNAY

NOTE. — The wines sold under the name "Volnay Santenots" come from the commune of Meursault.

Controlled Appellation : **Volnay.**

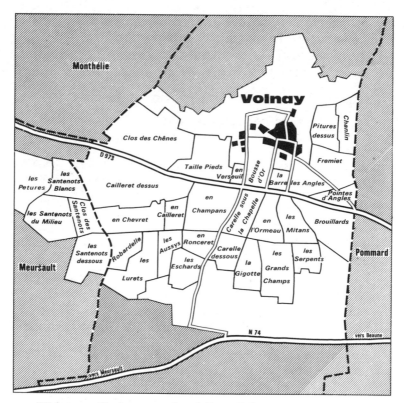

This appellation may be followed by :—

— either the expression "Premier Cru" or the name of the climat of origin in the case of those wines produced from the plots indicated in the list below ;

— or, just the name of the "climat" in the case of those wines from other plots (see p. 89).

Current list of classified "First Growth" climats :—

EN CAILLERETS, CAILLERETS-DESSUS, EN CHAMPANS, EN CHEVRET

Fremiets, Bousse-d'Or, La Barre or Clos-de-la-Barre, Le Clos-des-Chênes, Les Angles, Pointe-d'Angles, Les Mitans, En l'Ormeau, Taille-Pieds, En Verseuil, Carelle-sous-la-Chapelle, Ronceret, Carelle-Dessous, Robardelle, Les Lurets, Les Aussy, Les Brouillards, Les Clos-des-Ducs, Les Pitures-Dessus, Chanlin, Les Santenots (reds), Les Petures (reds), Village-de-Volnay.

— colour : red wines only ;
— boundary area : 242 ha 27 a (143 ha 97 a in first growths) ;
— minimum alcoholic strength : 10.5 degrees, First Growths 11° ;
— maximum yield : 40 hl/hectare ;
— average harvest : 7,300 hl ;
— reclassified : Bourgogne or Bourgogne Grand Ordinaire.

Appreciation : *The wines of Volnay, somewhat less coloured than those of Beaune and Pommard, are above all renowned for their elegance, delicate flavour, perfect balance and "nose". After those of Musigny they are the finest of the whole of Burgundy.* (Camille RODIER.)

Commune : MONTHELIE

Controlled Appellation : **Monthelie.**

This appellation may be followed by :—

— either the expression "Premier Cru" or the name of the climat of origin in the case of those wines produced from the plots indicated in the list below ;

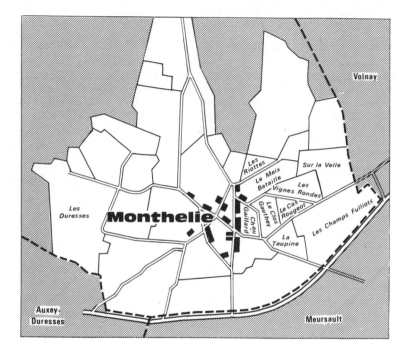

— or, just the name of the "climat" in the case of those wines from other plots (see p. 89).

Current list of classified "First Growth" climats :—

Sur Lavelle, Les Vignes-Rondes, Le Meix-Bataille, Les Riottes, La Taupine, Le Clos-Gauthey, Le Château-Gaillard, Les Champs-Fulliot, Le Cas-Rougeot, Duresse.

— colour : almost entirely red wines ;
— boundary area : 139 ha 90 a (31 ha 18 a in first growths) ;

— minimum alcoholic strength : reds 10.5, whites 11, First Growths red 11 degrees, white 11°5 ;
— maximum yield : red, 40 hl/hectare; white, 45 hl/hectare;
— average harvest : white wines, 65 hl ; red wines, 3,500 hl ;
— reclassified : red (see p. 164) ; white : Bourgogne or Bourgogne Grand Ordinaire.

Appreciation : *This wine is insufficiently known by consumers; it merits greater attention.* (VEDEL.)

Commune : AUXEY-DURESSES

Controlled Appellation : **Auxey-Duresses.**

This appellation may be followed by :—

— either the expression "Premier Cru" or the name of the "climat" of origin in the case of those wines produced from the plots indicated in the list below ;
— or, just the name of the "climat" in the case of those wines from other plots (see p. 89).

Current list of classified "First Growth" climats :—

Les Duresses, Les Bas-des-Duresses, Reugne, Reugne known as La Chapelle, Les Grands-Champs, Climat-du-Val known as Clos-du-Val, Les Écusseaux, Les Bretterins known as La Chapelle, Les Bretterins.

— colour : red and white wines ;
— boundary area : 169 ha 63 a (31 ha 76 a in first growths) ;

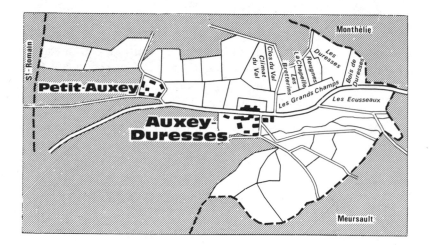

— minimum strength : reds 10.5, whites 11, First Growths red 11 degrees, white 11°5 ;

— maximum yield : red, 40 hl/hectare; white, 45 hl/hectare;

— average harvest : white wines, 1,100 hl; red wines, 3,600 hl;

— reclassified : red (see p. 164); white : Bourgogne or Bourgogne Grand Ordinaire.

Appreciation : *For a very long time (before the Appellation Laws) the wines of Duresses were sold as Volnay and Pommard without blemishing the reputation of these two great wines.* (Pierre-Léon GAUTHIER.)

Commune : *SAINT-ROMAIN*

Controlled Appellation : **Saint-Romain.**

— colour : red and white wines ;
— boundary area : 135 ha (no first growths) ;
— minimum strength : reds 10.5, whites 11 degrees ;
— maximum yield : red, 40 hl/hectare ; white, 45 hl/hectare ;
— average harvest : white wines, 1,200 hl ; red wines, 1,600 hl ;
— reclassified : red (see p. 164) ; white : Bourgogne or Bourgogne Grand Ordinaire.

Appreciation :

O Saint-Romain, bold, robust and so fruity
We like your freshness as much as your finesse.
(Roland Thévenin.)

Commune : *MEURSAULT*

Controlled Appellations :—

I. — **Meursault**

This appellation may be followed by :—

— either the expression "Premier Cru" or the name of the climat of origin in the case of those wines produced from the plots indicated in the list below ;
— or, just the name of the "climat" in the case of those wines from other plots (see p. 89).

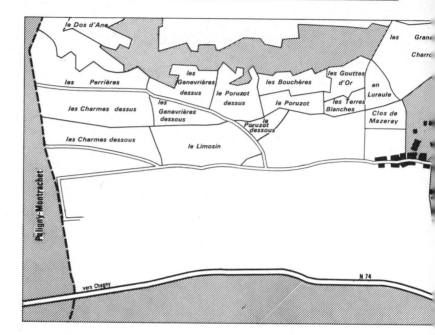

Current list of classified "First Growth" climats :—

AUX PERRIÈRES, LES PERRIÈRES-DESSUS, LES PERRIÈRES-DESSOUS
LES CHARMES-DESSUS, LES CHARMES-DESSOUS
LES GENEVRIÈRES-DESSUS, LES GENEVRIÈRES-DESSOUS

Le Poruzot-Dessus, Le Poruzot, Les Bouchères, Les Santenots-Blancs, Les Santenots-du-Milieu, Les Caillerets, Les Petures, Les Cras, La Goutte-d'Or.

AT BLAGNY : La Jennelotte, La Pièce-sous-le-Bois, Sous-le-dos-d'Ane.

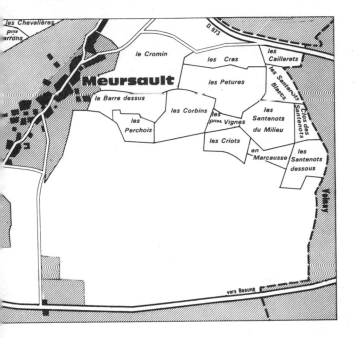

— colour : almost entirely white wines ;

— boundary area : 436 ha 82 a (131 ha 88 a in first growths) ;

— minimum alcoholic strength : reds 10.5, whites 11, First Growths reds 11 degrees, whites 11°5 ;

— maximum yield : red, 40 hl/hectare ; white, 45 hl/hectare ;

— average harvest : white wines, 14,700 hl ; red wines, 900 hl ;

— reclassified :—

red wines : see p. 164 ;
white wines : Bourgogne or Bourgogne Grand Ordinaire.

Appreciation : *The white wines of Meursault are both dry and mellow which is quite unusual. High in alcohol, a fine tint of greenish gold, brilliant and of good keeping qualities. With their "nose" of the ripe grape and flavour of hazel nuts they are classed as one of the most famous white wines of France.* (Camille RODIER.)

II. — **Volnay-Santenots** (see Volnay)

III. — **Blagny**

Only red wines produced in the hamlet of Blagny (located in between the appellations Puligny-Montrachet and Meursault) can claim for the appellation "Blagny" :

— colour : red wines ;
— boundary area : 54 ha 14 a (44 ha 41 a in First Growths) ;
— minimum alcoholic strength : reds 10.5° ;
— maximum yield : 40 hl/hectare ;
— average harvest : 260 hl ;
— reclassified : see page 145.

White wines coming from the same area are sold :

— either under the name of Meursault followed by the name of the climat (see above § I) ;
— or, under the name of Puligny-Montrachet (see further on).

Commune : *PULIGNY-MONTRACHET*

Controlled Appellations :—

I. — **Montrachet** (G.C.)
(partly in Chassagne-Montrachet)

— colour : white wines only ;
— boundary area : 8 ha 01 a ;
— minimum alcoholic strength : 12 degrees ;
— maximum yield : 40 hl/hectare ;
— average harvest : 316 hl ;
— reclassified : into Commune appellations of Puligny-Montrachet or Chassagne-Montrachet (whether First Growth or not) : Bourgogne or Bourgogne Grand Ordinaire.

Appreciation : *This admirable wine is the best white wine of Burgundy as Château-Yquem is in the Bordeaux region. They share the honour of being the two leading white wines of the world.* (BERTALL.)

II. — **Chevalier-Montrachet** (G.C.)
(all in Puligny-Montrachet)

— colour : white wines only ;
— boundary area : 7 ha 36 a ;
— minimum strength : 12 degrees ;
— maximum yield : 40 hl/hectare ;
— average harvest : 200 hl ;
— reclassified : Puligny-Montrachet (whether First Growth or not), Bourgogne or Bourgogne Grand Ordinaire).

III. — Bâtard-Montrachet (G.C.)
(partly in Chassagne-Montrachet)

— boundary area : 11 ha 86 a ;
— average harvest : 520 hl.

Bienvenues-Bâtard-Montrachet (G.C.)
(all in Puligny-Montrachet)

— boundary area : 3 ha 68 a ;
— average harvest : 160 hl.

Criots-Bâtard-Montrachet (G.C.)
(all in Chassagne-Montrachet)

— boundary area : 1 ha 57 a ;
— average harvest : 50 hl.

For these three wines :—

— colour : white wines only ;
— minimum alcoholic strength : 11.5 degrees minimum ;
— maximum yield : 40 hl/hectare ;
— reclassified :—

> *Bâtard-Montrachet :* see Montrachet ;
>
> *Bienvenues-Bâtard-Montrachet :* Puligny-Montrachet (whether First Growth or otherwise), Bourgogne or Bourgogne Grand Ordinaire ;
>
> *Criots - Bâtard - Montrachet :* Chassagne-Montrachet (whether First Growth or not), Bourgogne or Bourgogne Grand Ordinaire.

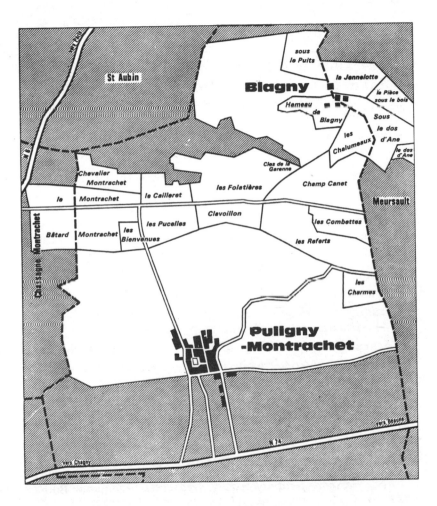

sous
le Puits

Blagny

le Jennelotte

le Pièce
sous le bois

Hameau
de
Blagny

Sous
le dos
d'Ane

St Aubin

les
Chalumeaux

le dos
d'Ane

Clos de la
Garenne

Chevalier
Montrachet

les Folatières

Champ Canet

Meursault

le Montrachet

le Cailleret

Chassagne-Montrachet

Bâtard Montrachet

les
Bienvenues

les Pucelles

Clavoillon

les Combettes

les Referts

les
Charmes

**Puligny
-Montrachet**

vers Chagny

N 74

vers Beaune

IV. — **Puligny-Montrachet**

This appellation may be followed by :—

— either, the term "Premier Cru" or the name of the climat of origin in the case of those wines produced from the plots indicated in the list below ;

— or, just the name of the "climat" in the case of those wines from other plots (see p. 89).

Current list of classified "First Growth" climats :—

LE CAILLERET, LES COMBETTES

Les Pucelles, Les Folatières, Clavoillons, Le Champ-Canet, Les Chalumeaux, Les Referts, Sous-le-Puits, La Garenne, Hameau-de-Blagny.

— colour : mainly white wines ;
— total area : 214 ha 34 a (100 ha 12 a in First Growths) ;
— minimum strength : 10.5° (red) and 11° (white), First Growths 11° (red) and 11.5° (white) ;
— maximum yield : red, 40 hl/hectare ; white, 45 hl/hectare ;
— average harvest : white wines, 9,300 hl ; red wines, 300 hl ;
— reclassified : red (see p. 164) ; white : Bourgogne or Bourgogne Grand Ordinaire.

Appreciation : *The best white wines are fruity, distinguished and of fine bouquet.* (Camille RODIER.)

The reds have plenty of body, a great finesse, and an exquisite bouquet develops with age. (DANGUY and AUBERTIN.)

Commune : *CHASSAGNE-MONTRACHET*

Controlled Appellations :—

I. — **Montrachet** (G.C.) (see Puligny-Montrachet)
II. — **Bâtard-Montrachet** (G.C.) (see Puligny-Montrachet)
Criots-Bâtard-Montrachet (G.C.) (see Puligny-Montrachet)

III. — **Chassagne-Montrachet**

This appellation may be followed by :—

— either the expression "Premier Cru" or the name of the climat of origin for those wines produced from the plots indicated on the list below ;
— or, just the name of the climat for those wines from other plots (see p. 89).

Current list of classified "First Growths" climats :—

CLOS-SAINT-JEAN, MORGEOT

Cailleret, en Remilly, Dent-de-chien, Vide-bourse.

La Maltroie, Les Chenevottes, Les Champs-Gain, Grandes-Ruchottes, La Romanée, Les Brussolles, Les Vergers, Les Macherelles, En Cailleret, Blanchot-Dessus, La Boudriotte, Bois-de-Chassagne, La Grande-Montagne.

— colour : more red wines than white wines ;
— total area : 338 ha 31 a (158 ha 79 a in First Growths) ;
— minimum strength : reds 10.5°, whites 11°, First Growths 11° (reds) and 11.5° (whites) ;

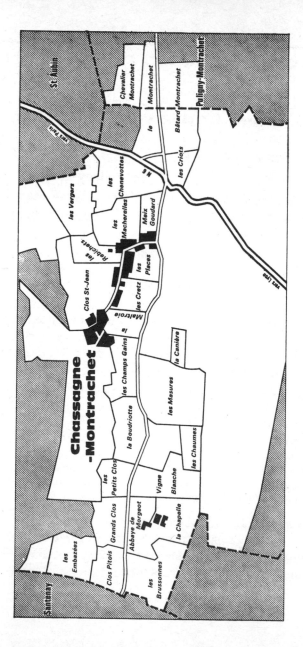

— maximum yield : red, 40 hl/hectare ; white, 45 hl/hectare ;
— average harvest : white wines, 5,800 hl ; red wines, 7,300 hl ;
— reclassified : red (see p. 164) ; white : Bourgogne or Bourgogne Grand Ordinaire.

Appreciation : *The red wines of Chassagne have an indisputable similarity to some of the great wines of the Côte de Nuits.* (Camille RODIER.)

Commune : SAINT-AUBIN

Controlled Appellation : **Saint Aubin.**

This appellation may be followed by :—

— either the expression "Premier Cru" or the name of the climat of origin for those wines produced from the plots indicated in on the list below ;
— or, just the name of the climat for those wines from other plots (see p. 89).

Current list of classified "First Growths" climats :—

Derrière-la-Tour, En Creot, Bas-de-Vermarain, Le Charmois, La Chatenière, Les Murgers-des-Dents-de-Chien, En Remilly, Les Frionnes, Sur-le-Sentier-du-Clou, Sur Gamay, Les Combes, Champlots, Village, Les Castets, Derrière-Chez-Edouard, Le Puits.

— colour : red and white wines ;
— boundary area : 236 ha 61 a (156 ha 46 a in First Growths) ;

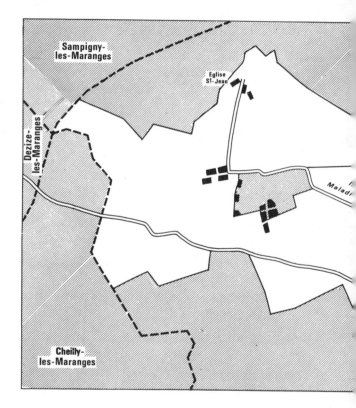

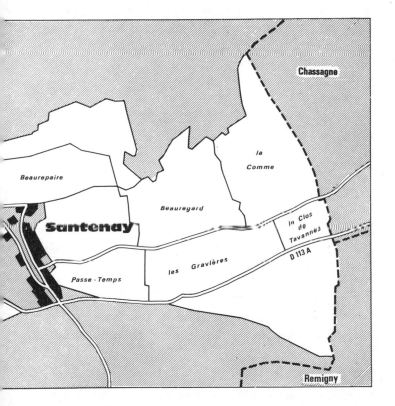

— minimum alcoholic strength : reds 10.5°, whites 11°. First Growths 11° (reds) and 11.5° (whites) ;
— maximum yield : red, 40 hl/hectare; white, 45 hl/hectare;
— average harvest : white wines, 1,050 hl; red wines, 2,300 hl;
— reclassified : red (see p. 164) ; white : Bourgogne or Bourgogne Grand Ordinaire.

Commune : *SANTENAY*

Controlled Appellation : **Santenay.**

This appellation may be followed by :—

— either the expression "Premier Cru" or the name of the climat of origin for those wines produced from the plots indicated in the list below ;
— or, just the name of the climat in the case of those wines from other plots (see p. 89).

Current list of climats are classified "First Growth" :—

LES GRAVIÈRES, CLOS-DE-TAVANNES, LA COMME

Beauregard, Le Passe-Temps, Beaurepaire, La Maladière, Clos-Rousseau.

— colour : mainly red wines ;
— boundary area : 407 ha 01 a (139 ha 78 a in First Growths) ;
— minimum strength : reds 10.5°, whites 11°, First Growths 11° (reds) and 11.5° (whites) ;
— maximum yield : red, 40 hl/hectare; white, 45 hl/hectare;

— average harvest : white wines, 200 hl; red wines, 12,000 hl;
— reclassified : red (see p. 164) ; white : Bourgogne or Bourgogne Grand Ordinaire.

Appreciation : *These are firm, velvety wines. They keep well and, with age, take on a very fine bouquet.* (Dr. LAVALLE).

Communes : CHEILLY, DEZIZE and SAMPIGNY-LES-MARANGES

Controlled Appellations : **Cheilly-les-Maranges, Dezize-les-Maranges and Sampigny-les-Maranges.**

These appellations may be followed by :—

— either the expression "Premier Cru" or the name of the climat of origin for those wines produced from the plots indicated in the list below ;
— or, just the name of the climat, in the case of those wines from other plots (see p. 89).

Current list of classified "First Growths" climats :—

COMMUNE OF CHEILLY-LES MARANGES
Les Maranges, Les Plantes-de-Maranges, La Boutière.

COMMUNE OF DEZIZE-LES-MARANGES
Les Maranges.

COMMUNE OF SAMPIGNY-LES-MARANGES
Les Maranges, Le Clos-des-Rois.

— colour : red and white wines ;
— boundary area : Cheilly 122 ha 41 a ; Dezize 66 ha 25 a ; Sampigny 41 ha 19 a ;

— minimum alcoholic strength : reds 10.5°, whites 11°,
  First Growths 11° for reds and 11.5° for whites ;

-- maximum yield : red, 40 hl/hectare; white, 45 hl/hectare ;

-- average harvest : fairly insignificant under these appellations ;

— reclassified : red (see below) ; white : Bourgogne or Bourgogne Grand Ordinaire.

Appellations : **Côte de Beaune-Villages**
and (Village's name followed by) **Côte de Beaune**

Only the red wines from any of the 16 appellations
given next can be marketed : Auxey-Duresses, Blagny, Chas-
sagne-Montrachet, Cheilly-les-Maranges, Chorey-les-Beaune,
Dezize-les-Maranges, Ladoix, Meursault, Monthélie, Pernand-
Vergelesses, Puligny-Montrachet, Saint-Aubin, Saint-Romain,
Sampigny-les-Maranges, Santenay, Savigny :—

— either under the name of these communes ;

— or under this name followed by "Côte de Beaune", for
  example "Auxey-Duresses Côte de Beaune", not to be
  confused with the appellation "Côte de Beaune" alone
  on the label ;

— or under the appellation "Côte de Beaune-Villages" ;

— or as "Bourgogne" or "Bourgogne Grand Ordinaire".

For these two appellations, the conditions of production
are those for the red wines of the villages where they come
from.

4. THE WINES OF THE SAONE-ET-LOIRE

A) The Mercurey Region

The Mercurey region is to the west of road No. 981, and stretches for about 15 miles between Chagny and Saint-Vallerin. It is sometimes called the "Côte Chalonnaise" as the vineyards are very near Chalon-sur-Saône. This town is now dedicated to industry, and no longer has any viticultural or vinicultural connections.

Here the outline of the hillsides no longer has the uniformity found in the Côte-d'Or. The vineyards still cling to the hills, but are less inclined to face east. The four principal appellations of Rully, Mercurey, Givry and Montagny are separated by meadows, field or thickets. Rully and Montagny at two opposite ends produce quite different white wines. The former is light and fruity and is used as a base for excellent sparkling Burgundy. The latter is more thrustful and has more bouquet and could be compared with certain Pouilly-Fuissé. One of the best "aligotés" in Burgundy is produced at Bouzeron near Chagny. In the centre of this region, Mercurey and Givry mainly make red wines which, in quality, rival those of the Côte de Beaune.

In fact, one again comes across the same type of climate and soil which characterises the Côte-d'Or. Furthermore it follows the same type of cultivation, vinification and marketing tradition, even the barrels have the same capacity, 225-228 litres, instead of 212-215 litre barrels used in the Mâconnais.

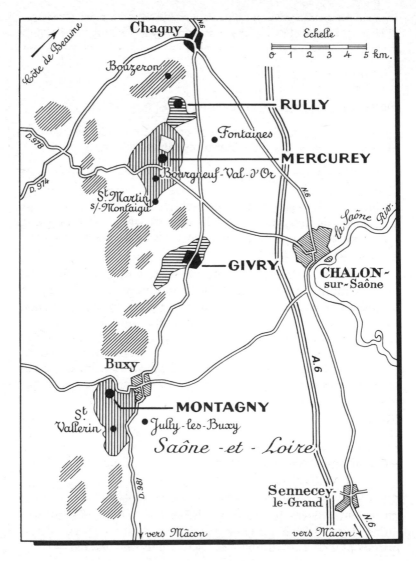

The Mercurey Region

Controlled Appellations :—

Mercurey.

This appellation can be followed by either the expression "Premier Cru" or the name of the "climat" of origin.

Clos-du-Roi, Clos-Voyen or Les Voyens, Clos-Marcilly, Clos-des-Fourneaux, Clos-des-Montaigus.

— colour : almost entirely red wines ;
— area : various plots of land in the Communes of Mercurey, Saint-Martin-sous-Montaigu, Bourgneuf-Val-d'Or ;
— minimum alcoholic strength : reds 10.5, whites 11, First Growths 11 degrees for red wines and 11.5 for white ;
— maximum yield : red, 40 hl/hectare ; white, 45 hl/hectare ;
— average harvest : white wines, 1,050 hl ; red wines, 21,500 hl ;
— reclassified : Bourgogne or Bourgogne Grand Ordinaire.

Appreciation : *The wine has body, bouquet, finesse and a distinction that resembles certain wines of the Côte de Beaune.*

Givry.

— colour : nearly all red wines ;
— minimum alcoholic strength : reds 10.5 degrees, whites 11 degrees ;
— maximum yield : red and white, 45 hl/hectare ;
— average harvest : white wines, 500 hl ; red wines, 4,900 hl ;
— reclassified : Bourgogne or Bourgogne Grand Ordinaire.

Appreciation : *A frank, rich wine, which, like Mercurey, is of the Côte de Beaune type.*

Rully.

This appellation may be followed by either the expression "Premier Cru" or the name of the "climat" of origin.

Margotey, Grésigny, Vauvry, Mont-Palais, Meix-Caillet, Les Pierres, La Bressande, Champ-Clou, La Renarde, Pillot, Cloux, Raclot, Raboursay, Écloseaux, Marissou, La Fosse, Chapitre, Préau, Moulesne.

— colour : mainly white wines ;
— minimum alcoholic strength : reds 10.5°, whites 11°, First
    Growths 11 for reds and 11.5 for whites ;
— maximum yield : white, 45 hl/hectare ; red, 40 hl/hectare ;
— average harvest : white wines, 3,200 hl ; red wines, 3,450 hl ;
— reclassified : Bourgogne or Bourgogne Grand Ordinaire.

Appreciation : *A very individual white wine which converts into a sparkling wine remarkably well. It was the base and foundation of the important sparkling wine business of this village.*

Montagny.

This appellation may be followed by either the expression the term "Premier Cru" or the name of the climat of origin.

— colour : white wines only ;
— boundary area : plots in the communes of Montagny, Buxy,
    Saint-Vallerin, and Jully-les-Buxy, 426 ha 41 a ;
— minimum alcoholic strength : 11 degrees and 11.5 for
    Premiers Crus ;

— maximum yield : 45 hl/hectare ;
— average harvest : 3,800 hl ;
— reclassified : Bourgogne or Bourgogne Grand Ordinaire.

Appreciation : *A white wine which freshens the mouth and keeps the head clear.*

B) The Mâconnais

The Mâconnais area lies in southern Burgundy in between Northern France and the South. Big sloping roofs covered with flat tiles give way to nearly Provençal roofs which are not so pointed and have incurved Roman type tiles. In the past, the dialect of Northern France finished here and the dialect of the South started. To-day, the Gamay has, in its turn, taken over from the Pinot.

The Mâconnais vineyards are situated in an immense trapezium of which the main base, formed to the East by the Route Nationale 6 from Sennecey-le-Grand to Crèches-sur-Saône measures 25 miles. The shorter base formed to the West by road No. 481 from Saint-Gengoux-le-National to Cluny is about 15 miles long and the overall depth averages 9 miles.

Here, one no longer finds a solid mass of vines which characterised the Côte-d'Or. The ground suitable for vine cultivation appears, where the soil, slopes and exposure are favourable, be it in the middle of the grassland, mixed cultivation or forestry. The climate, less harsh than in Northern Burgundy has changed the landscape and, in particular, the habitat. The villages, nearly all endowed with charming Romanesque Churches and balconied houses are especially quaint. The terrain, which starts with a series of gentle parallel hills,

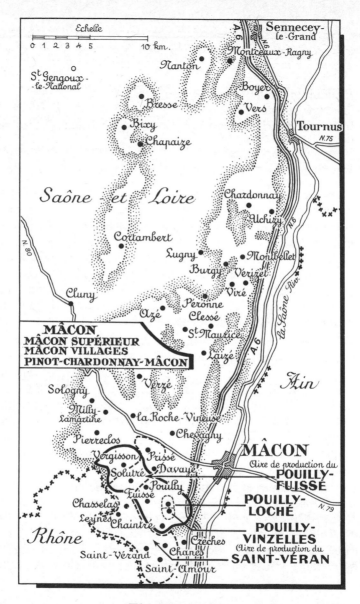

The Mâcon Area

becomes gradually more pronounced as one goes down towards the South. The country suddenly swells into vast geological waves, which are crowned with rocky formations. The most spectacular are the rocks of Vergisson and Solutré. It is on these proud slopes that the great white wines of viticultural Burgundy come from, namely, Pouilly-Fuissé.

The rest of the Mâconnais produces a large quantity of red wine, fruity and very pleasant when young. Also simple white wines which should be drunk when they still have all their freshness.

I

Pouilly-Fuissé.

This appellation may be followed by the name of the "climat" of origin :—

— colour : white wines only ;
— area of production : the communes of Fuissé, Solutré, Pouilly, Vergisson and Chaintré ;
— minimum alcoholic strength : 11° ; First Growths 12° ;
— maximum yield : 50 hl/hectare ;
— average harvest : 36,100 hl ;
— reclassified : Mâcon-Villages, Mâcon Supérieur, Mâcon Bourgogne or Bourgogne Grand Ordinaire.

Appreciation : *The wine of Pouilly-Fuissé charms the eye then delights the palate. Golden in colour with a tinge of emerald and vigorous as any of the great wines of Burgundy. Its dryness and freshness imparts a particularly seductive bouquet.*

Pouilly-Vinzelles and **Pouilly-Loché.**

These appellations may be followed by the name of the "climat" or the name place of origin :—

— colour : white wines only (Chardonnay vine) ;
— area of production : the Communes of Vinzelles and Loché ;
— minimum alcoholic strength : 11°, First Growths 12° ;
— maximum yield : 50 hl/hectare ;
— average harvest : Pouilly-Vinzelles : 2,000 hl and Pouilly-Loché, 1,200 hl ;
— reclassified : as Pouilly-Fuissé. Pouilly-Loché can be reclassified as Pouilly-Vinzelles but the contrary cannot be done.

Saint-Véran (1).

This appellation may be followed by the name of the climat or the name place of origin :

— colour : white wine only (Chardonnay vine) ;
— area of production : the following Communes in the Saône-et-Loire : Chânes, Chasselas, Davayé, Leynes, Prissé, Saint-Amour, Saint-Vérand and in Solutré : Section D Nos. 294 to 306, 322 to 341, except land, which by the nature of its soil and exposure, is unsuitable for producing appellation wine ;
— minimum alcoholic strength : 11°, with a climat 12° ;
— maximum yield : 55 hl/hectare ;
— average harvest : 13,500 hl ;

(1) Note : the name of the commune of Saint-Vérand is written with a d, the name of the appellation is written without a d.

— reclassified : Mâcon-Villages, Mâcon Supérieur, Mâcon, Bourgogne or Bourgogne Grand Ordinaire.

II. — Mâcon Supérieur
or Mâcon followed by the name of the Commune of Origin
Mâcon-Villages (white wines)

— area of production : defined areas in the communes around Mâcon and other different Communes. (The area of production is not the same for red and white wines and Mâcon-Villages.)

— colour : red and white wines. Possibility of rosé ;

— minimum alcoholic strength ; reds 10°, whites 11° ;

— maximum yield : red, 55 hl/hectare ; white, 60 hl/hectare ;

— average harvest : Mâcon Supérieur : white wines, 8,200 hl ; red wines, 13,000 hl. Mâcon-Villages (white) : 95,000 hl.

— reclassified :—

1. Mâcon plus the name of the Commune : *reds :* Mâcon Supérieur, Mâcon, Bourgogne Grand Ordinaire ; *whites :* Mâcon-Villages, Mâcon Supérieur or Mâcon, Pinot-Chardonnay-Mâcon, Bourgogne or Bourgogne Grand Ordinaire ;

2. Mâcon Supérieur : *reds :* Mâcon, Bourgogne if the wine is produced from the Pinot (proof required), Bourgogne Grand Ordinaire ; *whites :* Pinot-Chardonnay-Mâcon or Mâcon, Bourgogne, Bourgogne Grand Ordinaire ;

3. Mâcon-Villages : *whites :* Mâcon supérieur, Mâcon or Pinot-Chardonnay-Mâcon, Bourgogne, Bourgogne Grand Ordinaire.

NOTE. — The name Mâcon-Villages must NEVER be used for red wines.

III. — Mâcon
Pinot-Chardonnay-Mâcon (white wines)

The appellation Mâcon covers red and rosé wines made from the Gamay or Pinot grape.

White wines made from the Pinot blanc or the Chardonnay grape may take advantage of the appellation **Pinot-Chardonnay-Mâcon,** or Mâcon.

— area of production : see Mâcon Supérieur ;
— color : mainly reds, some white and rosé;
— minimum strength : reds 9°, whites 10° ;
— maximum yield : red, 55 hl/hectare ; white, 60 hl/hectare ;
— average harvest : white wines, 1,100 hl ; red wines, 2,600 hl ;
— reclassified : Bourgogne Grand Ordinaire.

General Appreciation : *The wines of the Mâconnais enjoy an important rôle in the range of the wines of Burgundy.*

Above all others are the excellent white wines of Pouilly whose solid qualities allow a large clientele to enjoy a typical good Burgundy.

Those white wines having the right to be called Mâcon-Villages or Mâcon Supérieur are frequently sold simply as white Burgundy and by this name are known throughout the world.

As for the red wines, they do not pretend to attain the qualities found in the Côte-d'Or, but they do fill their role as the advance-guard to the fine wines of Burgundy with honour. They are pretty robust and at their best when consumed quite young, as they do not improve very much with bottle age.

5. THE WINES OF THE RHONE
(VILLEFRANCHE DISTRICT)

Beaujolais

Whereas the way from the Chablis region to the Côte-d'Or, from the Côte-d'Or to the Mercurey region and from the last area to Mâconnais, was well defined, the route through the Mâconnais to Beaujolais is woolly and undetermined. The district of La Chapelle-de-Guinchay, where Chénas, Saint-Amour and Moulin-à-Vent come from (i.e. three great vineyards of Beaujolais), is, curiously enough, geographically situated in the Mâconnais.

The Beaujolais occupies a territory nearly similar in size to that of the Mâconnais, but there are more vineyards close on 16,000 hectares which is equal to about half the total A.O.C. area in Burgundy. Here the vine reigns supreme, right up to the summits of high hills, all wrinkled with small roads where one can enjoy getting lost like in a maze.

The granite soils which best suit the Gamay, are centred in the Northern part and give birth to the better known new vineyards. Around these vineyards, thirty six communes produce Beaujolais-Villages. In fact the Southern part is the spring-head of this large "river" called Beaujolais ; which served from the wood and carafe is the source of happiness, not only to the Lyonnais people, but to many Frenchmen and foreigners.

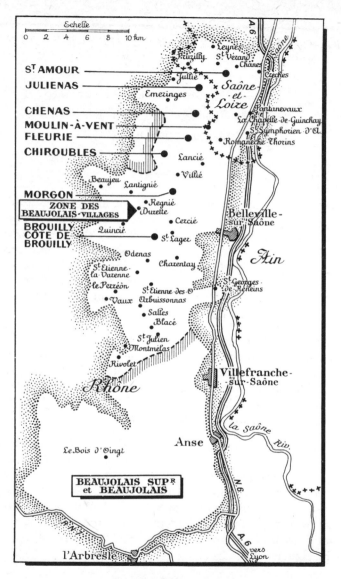

The Beaujolais Area

I. — The Growths of Beaujolais

BROUILLY :—
— area : some 800 ha ;
— average harvest : 67,400 hl.

CHÉNAS :—
— area : about 185 ha ;
— average harvest : 13,200 hl.

CHIROUBLES :—
— area : about 250 ha ;
— average harvest : 17,100 hl.

COTE DE BROUILLY :—
— area : about 200 ha ;
— average harvest : 16,000 hl.

FLEURIE :—
— area : about 700 ha ;
— average harvest : 42,000 hl.

JULIÉNAS :—
— area : about 530 ha ;
— average harvest : 30,700 hl.

MORGON :—
— area : 550 ha ;
— average harvest : 56,800 hl.

MOULIN-A-VENT :—

— area : about 700 ha ;
— average harvest : 35,000 hl.

SAINT-AMOUR :—

— area : about 215 ha ;
— average harvest : 14,800 hl.

For all these wines :—

— possibility of adding the name of the "climat" of origin to the name of the appellation (except for Brouilly) ;
— colour : red wines only ;
— minimum alcoholic strength : 10° (except Côte de Brouilly which is 10.5°), if coupled with the name of the "climat" 11° ;
— maximum yield : 48 hl/hectare ;
— reclassified : Bourgogne, Beaujolais-Villages, Beaujolais Supérieur, Beaujolais or Bourgogne Grand Ordinaire.

Note that "Côte de Brouilly" may not be reclassified to "Brouilly" neither may "Brouilly" be changed to "Côte de Brouilly".

II. — Beaujolais-Villages
or Beaujolais followed by the name of the village of origin

Area of production : The Communes of Juliénas, Jullié, Émeringes, Chénas, Fleurie, Chiroubles, Lancié, Villié-Morgon, Lantigné, Beaujeu, Régnié, Durette, Cercié, Quincié, Saint-Lager, Odenas, Charentay, Saint-Étienne-la-Varenne,

Vaux, Le Perréon, Saint-Étienne-des-Ouillères, Blacé, Arbuissonnas, Salles, Saint-Julié, Montmelas, Rivolet, Denicé, Les Ardillats, Marchampt, Vauxrenard, in the Department of the Rhône ;

And : Leynes, Saint-Amour-Bellevue, La Chapelle-de-Guinchay, Romanèche, Pruzilly, Chânes, Saint-Vérand, Saint-Symphorien-d'Ancelles in the Department of Saône-et-Loire.

— colour : almost entirely red wines with a possibility of white and rosé wines ;
— area : about 1,700 ha in addition to the growths or "crus" of Beaujolais mentioned under heading No. I on the two previous pages ;
— minimum alcoholic strength : reds 10°, whites 10.5° ;
— maximum yield : red, 50 hl/hectare ; white, 55 hl/hectare ;
— average harvest : white wines 820 hl ; red wines about 344,000 hl ;
— reclassified : Beaujolais Supérieur, Beaujolais or Bourgogne Grand Ordinaire.

III. — Beaujolais Supérieur
Beaujolais

— colour : almost entirely red wines (rosé and white wines are authorized) ;
— boundary area : those given in I and II above plus about 11,130 ha ;
— minimum alcoholic strength : Beaujolais ; red 9°, white 9.5° ; Beaujolais Supérieur ; red 10°, white 10.5° ;
— maximum yield : Beaujolais, 50 hl/hectare ; Beaujolais Supérieur, 55 hl/hectare ;

— average harvest : Beaujolais 521,000 hl (red)—2,000 hl (white) ; Beaujolais Supérieur 11,500 hl ;
— reclassified :—

> *Beaujolais Supérieur :* Beaujolais or Bourgogne Grand Ordinaire.

> *Beaujolais :* Bourgogne Grand Ordinaire.

Appreciation for all the wines of Beaujolais : *This is an opportunity for us to praise the "vin de carafe" for, above all, Beaujolais is the perfect wine to serve in this manner. The wine whose name is soft on the ear and gay on the palate.*

Beaujolais-Villages, your wines are loved because they are not great ; we can enjoy them young without impatiently waiting for them to mature. Moreover they possess a rare quality for a red wine—they may be drunk quite cool. (L. ORIZET.)

The fine and semi-fine wines of Beaujolais have delicacy and lightness but although not as rich in bouquet as the great wines of Upper Burgundy nevertheless have a fine perfume. Generally speaking they are quick to mature ; precocity is one of their distinctive characteristics. (Victor RENDU.)

CHAPTER VI

EAUX-DE-VIE
AND SPARKLING WINES

1. MARC DE BOURGOGNE

After vinification, skins and pips of both red and white grapes left over from the various pressings are usually kept for distillation.

Normally this operation takes place during the winter months, because not only has the vinegrower other worries on his hands during the harvest, but it was also found that skins and pips distilled immediately after pressing, produced an alcohol lower in strength and not so fine in quality.

The solid mass of skins and pips (marc or gennes, as it is known in Burgundy) is crumbled and carefully packed into vats (or open ended casks). These are sealed with a mortar of clay or fat and inspected at regular intervals. A natural drying process causes cracks in the mortar which has to be resealed from time to time. The marc undergoes a sort of slow fermentation, transferring the remaining sugar into alcohol.

During the winter months, a special mobile alambic still is made available in the villages by the Public Works under strict supervision of Government Inspectors, then the pips and skins *(marc)* are distilled. Vinegrowers in Burgundy are not permitted to distil privately.

The product obtained by this distillation is *Eau-de-Vie de Marc de Bourgogne* or more generally known as *Marc de Bourgogne*.

When the Marc de Bourgogne comes out of the alambic still, it should not exceed 71° in strength, but, in fact, it rarely exceeds 52°. In common with other Eau-de-Vie made from wine, it must mature for as long as possible in oak casks. In these containers, a slow evaporation takes place. Gradually the marc becomes round and smooth, at the same time drawing in a light caramel colour from the tannin in the oak. Ageing produces its quality and commercial value.

Marc de Bourgogne must be submitted to an official Tasters' Commission for approval before being sold. If the quality is satisfactory, the approved appellation is granted. In addition, as for all drinks, a strict legislation controls its production, bottling labelling, distribution and sale. In particular the alcoholic strength at the time of sale to the consumer must not be less than 40°.

Since April 1959, all Eaux-de-Vie sold to retailers and consumers had to be sold in bottles containing not more than three litres. In November 1973, a Ministerial Decree up-dated these regulations which are concerned with the harmonisation of container sizes.

From this date, it was decided that the Burgundy bottle used for Eau-de-Vie must contain 70 cl. net by volume.

But the seizure by the State of all production of alcohol during the war, coupled with the ever increasing taxes, plus the anti-alcohol campaign has diminished production, stocks and demand by alarming proportions. The principal consumers these days being the vine-growers themselves and a handful of overseas customers.

2. BURGUNDIAN BRANDY

Even more closely associated with the wine of Burgundy is the *Eau-de-Vie de Vin de Bourgogne* or *Fine Bourgogne* which is made from the direct distillation of wine.

In contrast to certain regions, such as Cognac and Armagnac, whose large quantities of unknown wines are distilled, the production of Eau-de-Vie in Burgundy is very limited and of no great commercial interest. The great demand for these fine wines makes it unnecessary for them to be sold in any other form. However, lees from the various rackings are used as a base. Eau-de-Vie produced from fresh unfiltered lees is as good as, and often more perfumed than, an Eau-de-Vie made directly from the wine.

Fine Bourgogne is subject to the same controls and regulations as Marc de Bourgogne. It is kept and aged under similar conditions. Sales are small for the same reasons that apply to Marc de Bourgogne.

3. CRÉMANT DE BOURGOGNE

SPARKLING BURGUNDY

During the first few years of the XIXth century experiments were made by a merchant in Nuits-Saint-Georges acquainted with the method champenoise at Rully in Saône-et-Loire (the white wines of this commune beeing particularly favourable for making sparkling wine).

These wines are commercialized under the appellation "Bourgogne Mousseux". The wine makers wanted to have a base wine specially vinified for the champagnization. This is why they issued a decree in 1975 to create the appellation "Crémant de Bourgogne".

The Crémant de Bourgogne is prepared as Champagne. It calls for long and exacting work. We remind you here of the essential steps :—

— harvest from the authorized varietals

    1st category : Pinot noir, Pinot gris, Pinot blanc, Chardonnay ;

    2nd category : Gamay noir à jus blanc, Aligoté, Melon, Sacy ;

    the finished product must have at least 30 % of 1st category varietals ;

— pressing carefully without mixing the wines from the final press ;

— filling the bottles and adding "liqueur de fermentation" ;

— remuage : turning the bottle to make the sediment slide
     down towards the neck of the bottle ;
— ageing in bottle for 9 months on their lees ;
— disgorging : expulsion of the impurities, the bottle is
     refilled with the "liqueur of expedition" ;
— finally corking and fixing the wire cap.

Today almost 5 millions bottles of Crémant de Bourgogne
are made, mostly in white and in rosé.

It is possible to produce red "Bourgogne Mousseux" from
still wines having the right to the appellation "Bourgogne"
but this production tends to be very marginal.

CHAPTER VII

THE WINE TRADE

I. THE PARTNERS OF THE PROFESSION

A) The vinegrowers

As we have already mentioned (Chapters II and III), the role of the vinegrower is cradled in both these provinces ; he is spared neither trouble nor anxiety. Cultivation, in some respects, calls for strength not only in the arm but also in the head ; coupled always with common sense. The risks of a greatly reduced or even non-existent harvest are always present from the moment the vine buds until the picking of the grapes. Unexpected Spring frosts, parasitical or crypto-gamic diseases, rain, lack of sun, storms and hail, all threaten the vine from April to September and can nullify the efforts and care of the best vinegrowers. In addition, as vines are the only crop grown in good viticultural areas, a poor year can become a financial disaster and the uncertainty of the following year antagonises the situation.

In the past for want of equipment, of "savoir-faire" or time, the vinegrower often sold his harvest to the wine merchants either as grapes as "new wine under the wine press" or "at the racking in March". Due to the smallness of his property and his small income the vinegrower could not afford the least investment and he had to sell his harvest.

One glance at these statistics demonstrates that the main characteristic of the Burgundian vineyard is the way in which it is split up into small parcels.

Because of this, viticulture in Burgundy does not play the same role as it does in the Bordeaux region where the statistics for the 1984 vintage show that there were 21,118 growers (against 37,386 in Burgundy) for 98,840 hectares of vines in production of which 82,642 hectares had the right to "appellation contrôlée" (against 41,470 hectares and 38,168 hectares in Burgundy).

In the Gironde, it is not rare to find quite a large vineyard, Château or a Domaine, owned by a single tenant. After the harvest the grower makes and bottles his own wine, puts it into cases and completes the whole cycle from the production to the sale. These wines are more readily known after the name of the property rather than the controlled appellation.

In Burgundy, the opposite prevails. Large estates are few and these are in the hands of wine merchants who are, at the same time, vinegrowers.

Properties are mainly composed of small plots and situated in various climats. The wine is sold under the one appellation by a great number of growers.

It is of interest to note, for example, that Chambertin is shared by 25 growers, Clos de Vougeot by 75, Montrachet by 13, etc. In the case of other growths, the number is in about the same proportions.

Not long ago, most of the vinegrowers did only the cultivation of the wine and the vinification. Now, with the modernisation of the means of cultivation, the crowds of tourists in the viticultural regions and the infatuation of wine lovers for wines coming straight from the property, the vinegrowers, especially in Côte-d'Or, commercialize part of their production. Today the sales straight from the property represent about 20 % of the harvest in Burgundy.

B) The country winebrokers

Due to the large number of producers scattered over a wide area, there has to be a link between them and the wine merchants.

Quite frequently, the heads of commercial firms do not have the time to seek out the wines they require. Many of their purchases are made after tasting samples sent in by the country winebrokers or *courtiers de campagne*.

These brokers, situated in the heart of the vineyards, explore well defined sectors and submit to the wine merchants those wines which they think may be of interest to them. After the sale has been made, they keep a watching brief on behalf of their client while the wine is racked, arrange for delivery and sometimes supervise the payment. Formerly they were remunerated by a fixed sum "per barrel"; to-day they receive a percentage of the price of the purchase.

An efficient and conscientious broker rends an important service both to commerce and viticulture. The rules governing the profession of "Country winebroker" has been regulated by the law of 31st December 1949.

C) The wine merchants
The export trade

At the beginning of the XVIIIth century the first business houses were founded in Burgundy (see p. 22) not only to meet the needs of the French market but equally to satisfy demands from Belgium and Flanders. Even to-day few merchants concentrate entirely on the home market. So it is difficult to speak about Burgundian trade without spending most of the time talking about exports.

Whereas the numerous small properties concentrated on production, the merchants gradually developed the sale and reputation of the wines of Burgundy abroad. They selected certain growths, nursed (1) them, and left them to age in their cellars. Bonds of friendship quickly formed between exporters and importers. Confidence was gained through deals, which then became routine and, finally, a tradition was established. The same rules of courtesy and loyalty still apply to this relationship.

---

(1) The French term for a wine merchant who buys young wine nursing it until it is mature for sale is called a *négociant-éleveur*.

In order to arrive at these results, the merchants dealing in the fine wines of Burgundy, have to overcome a number of obstacles. We have seen that nobody becomes an "éleveur" overnight. In addition to long technical experience, considerable investment in equipment is involved, recruitment of a large staff, and a profound knowledge is also required, coupled with frequent contacts with foreign buyers.

Success, however, has crowned these efforts because nearly 90 % of the export sales are now made by the way of Burgundian merchants who only number some 170 from the main centres : Belleville-sur-Saône, Villefranche-sur-Saône, Mâcon, Meursault, Savigny, Aloxe-Corton, Nuits, Dijon, Chablis, etc., and, of course, Beaune, the veritable capital of viticulture and viniculture.

In the French market, customers are solicited by agents or representatives. These are remunerated on a commission based on turnover figures. Depending on the region they call on either wholesalers, retailers or consumers. Very few firms specialise in one particular type of clientele.

So far as foreign markets are concerned, sales are generally made through a buying agent for the country in question. A newly-established exporter must have considerable patience, perseverance and deftness ; efforts can be disappointing to a beginner. In all impartiality, it must be recognised that those firms that obtain the best results are the "traditional firms", that is, those which have, for a very long time, been established in a market, which often, they themselves created.

No statistics reveal accurately the sales of Burgundy wines on the home market.

So far as exports are concerned, however, official figures are available to make a number of comparisons.

Thus the production of the vineyards of Burgundy represents these last few years, 13 % of the whole French production of controlled appellation wines ; that of Bordeaux, 24 % and all the others appellations together, 63 %.

Taking into account these percentages, Burgundy exports proportionally more than the other regions. In 1986 Burgundy represents 22 % by volume of the total A.O.C. wines whereas the Bordeaux figure was 30 %, Côtes du Rhône, 13 %, Champagne, 8 %. By value the percentage for these same regions are : Burgundy, 24 % ; Bordeaux, 25 % ; Côtes du Rhône, 7 % and Champagne, 31 %.

These exports are divided between more than 170 countries (see details p. 233).

Up until 1971, Burgundy exported more wine in cask than in bottle, but since 1972 it is the contrary. Since about ten years ago this progression of exports has been due to the sales in bottle, the sales in cask staying stable. In 1986 the sales in bottle reached 79 % of the volume and 89 % of the value of all exports.

The proportion of the exports in bottle vary considerably according to the country. For all A.O.C. wines in 1986, Switzerland and Sweden take about 39 % of their wine from us in this form, Great Bretain and Canada, 85 %, Germany, 90 % and the U.S.A., 100 %.

We have tried to make these unappealing figures more meaningful and in the last pages of this book we have made graphs of :—

— the exportations of the A.O.C. wines of Burgundy from 1952 to 1986 by volume ;
— the exportations of the A.O.C. wines of Burgundy from 1952 to 1986 by value ;

and we have given the statistics of the exportations in 1986 to all the countries of the world. We suggest that you refer to it.

***

In spite of these spectacular results, the increase in exports is not carried out independently. For each country there are special regulations, making it highly complicated to the exporter, frequently limiting his potentialities.

As an example, we show next the principal difficulties encounted for fourteen countries representing in 1986 more than 95 % of the total exports of Burgundy.

Switzerland. — Sales on a quota basis ; import licences mainly granted to Swiss whole salers, very small annual quota for individuals and retailers (10,000 hl).

West Germany, Belgium, Denmark, Great Bretain, Luxembourg, Holland, Irland and Italy. — Sales allowed to all clientele and Common Market regulations.

U.S.A. — No quotas but sales may only be made to holders of import permits. No possibility of despatches to individuals, even as gifts.

— 193 —

Sweden, Norway, Finland. — Each of these countries has a state monopoly which is the sole buyer and distributor of wines.

Canada. — A governmental commission exists in each province for the purchase and sale of all wines.

D) The interprofessional committees

At all times, the persons in charge of the viticulture and the wine trade meet to debate the problems of the A.O.C. of Burgundy. From these meetings the following interprofessional committees were created (1) :—

— the "Union interprofessionnelle des Vins du Beaujolais" in 1959 (U.I.V.B.) ;
— the "Comité interprofessionnel de Saône-et-Loire" for the Controlled Appellation of Origin of Burgundy and Mâcon in 1963 (C.I.B.M.) ;
— the "Comité interprofessionnel de la Côte-d'Or et de l'Yonne" for the Controlled Appellation of Origin of Burgundy in 1966 (C.I.B.).

The interprofessional committees bring together at parity the representatives of the professional organisations of the viticulture and of the trade. The missions untrusted to them concern : the promotion of the appellations of which they take charge of on the domestic and international market, the basic and applied technical research which leads them to create or

(1) The interprofessional committees' addresses are given on page 245.

control the laboratories and lastly, in the economic field, the knowledge of supply and demand, the adaptation of the supply to the demand and the use of market regulations under state control.

In Burgundy to take in consideration the interdependence of the economic problems of the viticultural region, the three basic interprofessional associations created the F.I.V.B. (Fédération des Interprofessions viticoles de Grande Bourgogne) to delegate to it their missions in this field.

The ressources of the interprofessionals are derived from a tax and a volontary subscription fixed by the professionals. Through the meeting between the partners of the profession, the interprofessional associations are the expression of their desire to adapt production to an outside world in constant change.

2. COMMERCIAL BRANDS AND
"VINS DE MARQUE"

Before the war of 1914-1918 only certain names of growths or villages were known to the public both at home and abroad. They had been chosen as traditional ensigns for the wines of Burgundy. Some countries still do not respect our appellations and use the names to describe types of wine totally foreign to our region.

At the time of the introduction of the appellations (1919) many villages (sometimes individual proprietors) tried to impose their "Growths" without regard to local customs and loyalties or even commercial viability. This individualism multiplied the number of controlled appellations, and, therefore, the areas of production had to be defined and enforced.

These wines whose names had been formerly "launched" were, therefore, at an advantage and sold readily; some of them too easily. On the other hand, the vinegrowers and merchants experienced greater difficulty in selling other wines which had frequently received greater care but were unknown to the buyer.

Moreover, because the quantity of each appellation became more restricted and the quality varied according to the vintage, it was frequently impossible to offer regular supplies to the customers.

All these reasons incited the commercial people of Burgundy to adopt the system which had succeeded in Champagne and Cognac, where the brand is certainly the best guarantee to the customer. The same system is used in the Bordeaux region where the "domaine" or Château can be considered as a commercial brand.

Many merchants, therefore, register their special brands in order to sell certain wines which they have carefully nurtured and whose quality is the best guarantee of their reputation.

These wines are naturally subject to the laws governing Controlled Appellations.

Wines sold under the name of a brand are always linked with a generic appellation defining their origin such as : Bourgogne.

As a rule these wines generally consist of a selection and blending of :—

— either declassified growths ;
— or, a good quality "Growth" whose name is little known to the consumer ;
— or, a mixture of these two types of "Growths" ; trial blends having been determined by tasters before hand.

⁎⁎*⁎*

Some merchants also offer to their customers *Vins de Marque* which are wines sold without stating their origin and, therefore, giving no guarantee of where they have come from.

Such wines are selected and blended aiming at a quality or price dictated by the consumer. So far as Burgundy is concerned, the wines are carefully matured as if they were entitled to the full appellation.

A special legislation is imposed on these *Vins de Marque* ; movement permits are on coarse paper (green paper for wines of appellation of origin, see p. 81), there are specific regulations governing labels (they must be different from those used for controlled appellation wines) ; special invoices and pricelists (they must not appear among wines of Controlled Appellation but must be shown either before or after these), etc.

Restaurants and hotels should always enter these "Vins de Marque" under the heading "Various Wines" on their wine lists and never under, for example, Burgundy, which is a controlled appellation.

3. VINTAGES

The main desire of the wine lover is to procure wines of good years and *better vintages*. In order to achieve this ambition he is frequently deluded by classifications, the value of which tends to be indicative rather than a hard and fast rule.

It is, in fact, too simple to catalogue the vintage years. One says that a certain year was excellent, good, mediocre or poor ; each of these qualities only sums up the *general tendency* of the year as many elements can contradict the reputation. All the vines may not be of the same age or have the same exposure. They may not be subjected to identical methods of cultivation and treatment. Not all vinegrowers pick their grapes at the most favourable moment and, above all, vinification does not take place under the same conditions.

So many vines, so many vinegrowers, so many wines. It is understandable, therefore, why mediocre wines are to be found in great vintage years and conversely, excellent wines in bad years. The Burgundian critic Albert Thibaudet quite correctly stated : *There are no good wines, there are only good bottles.* All the more reason for a wine lover to select a capable and conscientious supplier.

To begin with here are some past good years :—

— *from 1900 to 1949* : 1904, 1906, 1907, 1911, 1915, 1919, 1921, 1923, 1926, 1928, 1929, 1933, 1934, 1937, 1938, 1947, 1949.

Next we give the *average characteristics* (listed below) of more recent vintages without fear of being too misleading :

1947 : very hot year, vinification quite difficult. The 1947's which succeeded were of very high class.

1957 : small harvest but quite successful, making good bottles both red and white.

1958 : very abundant year. The white wines are classified as good. The reds require carefully choosing.

1959 : this harvest of record quantity (especially in the Côte-d'Or and in Saône-et-Loire) was acclaimed by the journalists as the vintage of the century. Supple and well-coloured wines but of somewhat irregular quality ranging from very good to average.

1960 : large harvest, especially in Beaujolais. Generally the wines are of weak constitution and must be chosen with care.

1961 : quite a large harvest. Wines full of breed and good constitution ; good bottles.

1962 : large harvest in the Côte-d'Or and Saône-et-Loire, a record in the Yonne but low in Beaujolais. Wines generally fruity are agreeable, supple and fine.

1963 : a very abundant year, quality varied considerably.

1964 : a very large harvest, a good vintage.

1965 : moderate quantity in general and below the average for the Côte-d'Or. The wines from this very late harvest are light, have little colour and should be drunk as soon as possible.

1966 : a very abundant year, a good vintage.

1967 : average quantity and quality except in Beaujolais where the quality of the wines were better.

1968 : a wet year, average quantity except in Beaujolais where it was big, great variation of quality from one grower to another and from one appellation to another. White wines in general better than reds.

1969 : good year, average harvest.

1970 : a very plentiful vintage in all the regions, very good quality.

1971 : quality wines good for keeping. Quantity normal in Beaujolais, irregular elsewhere and showing a shortage in the Côte-d'Or.

1972 : good enough year for quality, but the red wines are closed and need to be kept for a fairly long time to soften. As for the white wines, they are rather frail. Quantity is clearly above the average.

1973 : very large quantity. The biggest since the Controlled Appellations were introduced. The quality varies from quite good to mediocre depending on the area and the domaines.

1974 : average quantity and quality.

1975 : small quantity. Quality generally mediocre except for the white wines from the Côte-d'Or.

1976 : very early harvest after an exceptionally dry and warm spring and summer. A large crop. Quality of a great year.

1977 : quite a large harvest. Quality mediocre.

1978 : small quantity. Very high class.

1979 : a very abundant year. Red wines are distinguished; a good vintage for white wines.

1980 : average quantity. Red wines and white wines require carefully choosing.

1981 : a very small harvest. Average quality but some happy surprises.

1982 : the harvest of record quantity. Irregular quality ranging from very good to average, with rapport difficulties during vinification, particularly in Beaujolais.

1983 : quantity above the average, the wines look good enough but sometimes lack breeding.

1984 : quantity below the average, quality varied from average to mediocre with however some beautiful success in reds.

We would like to emphasise that the above appreciations are only *a reminder* of the characteristics of the vintages and, above all, are only valid during *the first few years* following the harvest.

The quality of the wines varies during their ageing in bottle; it is, in fact, always risky to pronounce judgment on a bottle of such-and-such Growth and of such-and-such vintage without having first tasted it.

4. NON-VINTAGE AND V.S.R. WINES

Vintage years were sometimes a trap into which the consumer fell, so the Burgundian merchant adopted the custom as practised in Champagne by offering to his client *non-vintage wines*, in addition to wines of a specific vintage.

These non-vintage wines are, generally speaking, a careful selection from vintages not enjoying a high reputation. They can also be a harmonious blend of "Growths" of identical origin but of different years, giving well balanced wines of regular and continuous quality.

The *Comité professionnel du Bourgogne* has created the abbreviation *V.S.R.* (very specially recommended) and merchants of our region can offer their wines under this banner.

A large number of merchants and even vinegrowers, in the rest of France (especially in Bordeaux), have asked for permission to use this title. It is freely granted on the condition that the quality of the wines is worthy of it.

Chapter VIII

THE WINE CELLAR
AND THE TABLE

The study of the culture of vines, vinification, the raising of wine and its character are, without doubt, the best introduction to the knowledge of wine. But the wine lover must still acquire some practical notions on how to place the wines in the best conditions for their appreciation. It is not our intention in these few pages to teach the wine lover how to drink ; we will confine ourselves to set out certain essential principles for the good presentation of Burgundy wines.

I. PURCHASE AND SERVING OF WINE

Before serving the wines and drinking them, it is necessary to buy them and to stock them appropriately.

In the past the wine lovers often bought their wines in casks and bottled their wines themselves. Today it is better and easier to buy the great wines in bottles.

Bottling becoming general in Burgundy, the wine lover can get his supply in different places : from the wine-grower, the proprietor or the wine-merchant, in the many small cellars open in the villages, in the cooperative stores or retailstores. It is better to have no preconceived ideas about the wine and to follow ones inclination : to profit from chance and visit a wine-merchant's cellar or a proprietor's vineyard for example. The wine-growers or proprietors never have a large choice of appellations but they sell their own wines. However the retailers or the wine-merchants have a large selection of appellations at different prices which they have already selected for their clients, wines of quality one can trust if they run a prosperous business. Finally it is good to know that the appellations of high renown always attain the highest prices.

After buying the bottles, it is necessary to have a cellar for stocking and ageing if needed. As a matter of fact the great wines are sold younger and younger for profitability reasons, although, they usually need to stay a few years in bottle to reach their full potential. This cellar, necessarily underground, must be planned away from light and vibrations and kept at a constant temperature (10°-14 °C). It is possible now to buy some "apartment cellars" with a special air conditioning system design for the preservation and ageing of wines.

Noblesse oblige... As the wealthy man should know how to spend money, so should the fortunate owner of great wines know how to serve them.

Many enthusiasts, full of good intentions, learn by heart that certain dishes should be accompanied by specific wines ; but this rigid rule can sometimes present embarrassing situations : either they may have the wine but are unable to prepare the dish or they have the dish but not the wine. True, there is an art in marrying wine to food but, nevertheless, this is controlled by certain rules that should always be followed if one is to avoid "discords" or dangerous liaisons.

WHITE AND ROSÉ WINES should be drunk cold but not iced. Many experts say that the temperature should be between 42 and 52 degrees Farenheit but it is usually equally satisfactory to bring the wine straight from the cellar at the time of serving. When two or more white wines are offered it is customary to serve the stronger or more full-bodied wine after the lighter one. These wines accompany soups, fish, shellfish, etc.

RED WINES should be consumed at room temperature but definitely not warm. The same experts advise 50 to 65 degrees Farenheit for red Burgundy. In practice, all that is required is to place the wine in the room in which it is to be served a few hours in advance and away from any form of direct heat. These wines accompany red meat, game and cheese ; the lighter wines being served before the more robust, bearing in mind the gastronomic law : *Never let the bottle you are drinking make you regret the one that came before it.*

With these general rules in mind we give below, merely as a guide, a short list of "marriages" for certain dishes to a few of the wines of Burgundy :—

Apéritif : Vin blanc Cassis, threequarters Bourgogne Aligoté and one quarter black currant liqueur.

Hors-d'œuvre, soups : white Mâcon, white Burgundy.

Oysters : Chablis, Pouilly-Fuissé.

Fried fish : Chassagne-Montrachet, Puligny-Montrachet.

Fish in sauce, lobsters : Meursault, Corton-Charlemagne, Montrachet.

Entrées : Santenay, Savigny, Chassagne, Beaujolais.

Meats with white sauce, poultry : Volnay, Beaune, Aloxe-Corton. Chambolle-Musigny.

Meats with dark gravy, roasts : Pommard, Nuits-Saint-Georges.

Game : Corton, Clos de Vougeot and all the great growths.

Cheeses : the more robust and full bodied wines such as Chambertin and Musigny.

Sweets, fruit, ices : Sparkling Burgundy, Crémant de Bourgogne.

Salads and dishes containing vinegar : no wine.

Coffee : Marc de Bourgogne, Burgundy Brandy.

(Remember that tobacco and smoke are enemies of wine.)

Before serving the chosen wines the corks must be carefully drawn. The *capsules* should be cut just above the ring on the neck of the bottle and this carefully wiped.

The choice of cork-screw is important as the cork should come out slowly without shaking the bottle. It is therefore advisable to use, for example, the "Rustic type." which have the screw set in a piece of vine wood or even a cork-screw attached to a waiter's knife, which can penetrate the whole length of the cork.

The *glasses* should be of clear glass, thin and of tulip shape in order to assist in the rotation of the wine and the concentration of the bouquet.

As to how to drink, this has been taught to us by the admirable words of one of our Great Men who, on noticing, that the person next to him at table had just emptied his glass in one large gulp exclaimed :—

Sir, when one has the honour and fortune to drink such a great wine as this ; one first of all looks at it, then inhales it, then tastes it... then one talks about it.

2. THE BURGUNDIAN CUISINE

By the glory of its vineyards, wrote Curnonsky, *by the richness of its soil, by the excellence and quality of its natural produce as well as the talent and taste of its chefs and Cordons Bleus who, for centuries, have maintained the highest traditions, Burgundy has become a gastronomic paradise.*

In fact, the Burgundian cuisine whose reputation extends beyond our frontiers, is renowned more for its simplicity and rustic atmosphere than for its refinements. Instead of listening to learned masters, one only hears the inexhaustible chatter between knife and fork. Since time immemorial, the Burgundians have been heavy eaters, gourmets and gourmands. It is their huntsman's temperament that makes them such happy companions on long walks and at heavy meals. They show no enthusiasm for snacks that only lie to the palate and deceive the stomach, preferring substantial dishes that fill the mouth and warm the tummy.

In addition to the renowned and scientifically trained chefs of France who carry our standard overseas, the Burgundian cuisine is above all represented by its modest cooks. They prepare the family dinners which are the very basis of the Burgundian reputation in an inimitable manner inherited from their grand-parents.

Good wine calls for a good dish, said Roupnel, *and sauces have an age old understanding with vineyards.* Wine, in fact, is one of the "raw materials" of the Burgundian kitchen. It not only accompanies the dishes, it marinates them, it scents them, colours them, soaks and cooks them. Sometimes even, when converted into humble vinegar or a spicy mustard, it seasons them.

It would be tedious to quote all the various dishes of Burgundy but now that our mouths are watering, we name those which, in our opinion, are the most representative of the region :—

— les Escargots de Bourgogne ;

— la Potée bourguignonne, le Cochon de lait à la Dijonnaise, le Porcelet en gelée au Chablis, le Jambon braisé à la lie de vin, le Jambon persillé ;

— le Bœuf bourguignon, la Daube bourguignonne, le Gigot d'agneau Bretonnières, les Paupiettes de veau au Pernand ;

— la Fricassée de poulet au Meursault, le Coq au Chambertin, le Civet de lapin à la Bourguignonne, le Râble de lièvre à la Piron, les Gibelottes au vin blanc, le Salmis de canard à la Gabriel, les Grives des vignes à la Jean-sans-Peur ;

— la Pauchouse de Verdun, le Brochet du Doubs, les Quenelles de brochet à la Fagon, les Tanches au bleu, les Meurettes, les Matelotes ;

— les Fromages de Cîteaux, d'Epoisses, la Gougère auxerroise ;

— le Pain d'épice de Dijon, blackcurrant desserts, etc.

In conclusion we say, with Georges Rozet, *it is in Burgundy that the art of eating and drinking well is at its harmonious best.*

CHAPTER **IX**

WINE FESTIVITIES

Since olden times, since the festivals of Dionysus and the Bacchanales, wine has never ceased to be the object of cults and festivals which over the centuries have recognised man's need for this drink.

All our wine regions possess a rich folk-lore which inspires both the vine and wine. But Burgundy, the Burgundy of "happy children" who are proud of their name, devotes special attention to "Monseigneur le Vin" and each year draws enthusiastic crowds of Wine lovers to the numerous festivities.

We will try to introduce you to a few of them.

"LES TROIS GLORIEUSES"

A) The Wine Sale of the Hospices de Beaune (1)

This is the most famous and traditional of all Burgundian manifestations. First started in 1850 when 189 barrels of fine wines were sold realising a total of F 19,247.50.

The sale is always held on the third Sunday in November in the unique setting of the "Hostel-Dieu" of Beaune.

To-day, the new wine coming from many different properties by generous donors is put up for auction at the Hospice de Beaune (Hôtel Dieu and Hospice de la Charité).

The "Hotel-Dieu" was founded under the name of "Hospital Saint-Antoine" on the 4th August 1443 by Nicolas Rolin, then Chancellor to Philippe le Bon, duke of Burgundy, and his wife Guigone de Salins "for occupation by the sick and needy".

Built by a Flemish architect, Jacques Viscrère, it has conserved, in spite of many political upheavals, not only its artistic authenticity but also its original intentions. Its "Dames Hospitalières" have never ceased, even in the most troubled times, to devote themselves to the service of the sick and poor (2).

---

(1) All enquiries for information should be addressed to : Office du Tourisme de Beaune, tél. : (80) 22.24.51. Hospices de Beaune, tél. (80) 22.53.53.
(2) During the French Revolution the Hotel-Dieu was called "the Hospital of Humanity" and the nursing sisters became citizens under the direction of Citizen Cécile Boileau.

Recently, after the construction of a new hospital which was opened by the President G. Pompidou in 1971, the Hôtel-Dieu became a museum. Here one can admire superb buildings, dating back to the Middle Ages, the famous polyptique of the *Last Judgment* by the early Flemish painter Roger Van der Weyden ; a magnificent wooden sculpture of the xvth century ; un *Christ à la pitié*, larger than life-size, still covered with the original colours and, finally, a beautiful collection of tapestries coming from various periods.

The vineyards of the Hospices which cover some hundred acres are divided between the main communes of the Côte de Beaune. The wines produced follow the same rules as the controlled appellation but the name "Hospices de Beaune" coupled with the name of the Cuvée are stated and appear on the labels.

This auction "the largest sale for charity in the world" brought in about 16 million francs in 1984 for the 636 pieces and one feuillette of wine sold. It offers practical assistance to sick people, aged people and needy invalids. In addition it helps purchase new equipment for the hospital, create a retirement home with medical care for the elderly and restore old buildings.

Many activities take place at the same time as the sale ; a general exhibition of all the wines from Burgundy, an exhibition of viticultural and vinification equipment and many other attractions.

The festivities end with a large candle-lit dinner in the old bastions of the Hôtel-Dieu and constitutes, along with the Chapter of the Brotherhood of Chevaliers du Tastevin (on the

Saturday evening) and the Paulée de Meursault (at noon on the Monday), the *Three Glorious Days of Burgundy*, known as *Les Trois Glorieuses de Bourgogne*.

B) THE CHAPTERS OF THE BROTHERHOOD
OF THE CHEVALIERS DU TASTEVIN (1)

The Brotherhood of the Chevaliers du Tastevin is the most famous and active of all wine societies. It holds a number of "Chapters" each year in the venerable Cistercian cellars of the Château du Clos de Vougeot (2) which were built by the monks of Cîteaux.

The oldest part (circa 1150) consists of two buildings. The first still shelters the four original wine presses whose imposing size and remarkable conservation are the admiration of all visitors. One of these presses is commissioned into use each year at the opening of the *Chapitre des Vendanges* to the great pleasure of all who are invited to the ceremony. The second building was the cellar in which new wine was stored ; now it serves as a background or stage for the manifestations of the Brotherhood.

The most recent part, the Château itself, dates from the Renaissance (1551). It served as a resting place for the Priors of Cîteaux when they stayed at the Clos.

The Château remained the property of the monks of Cîteaux until 1791. On the 17th January 1793, it was declared state

---

(1) For all information contact : Secrétariat de la Confrérie at Nuits-Saint-Georges (Côte-d'Or). Tél. : (80) 61.07.12.
(2) Guided tour every day.

property and sold. It saw many changes before passing to the ownership of the Confrérie which undertook its complete restoration.

All the Chapters are quite remarkable. They have charmed, conquered and regaled the highest and the most diverse personalities of the whole world. The picturesque and humorous harangues are inspired directly from Rabelais and Molière. In spite of the animated drinking songs of the Cadets of Bourgogne and the overflowing glasses, these wine functions always offer good entertainment, where courtesy and decency are never abused.

Certain Chapters are more dedicated to vinous traditions than others. These are : Saint-Vincent, The Harvest and the "Trois Glorieuses".

The *Saint-Vincent* celebrations, patronised by the Brotherhood, are organised on the first Saturday following the 22nd January, the feast of saint Vincent, patron Saint of Vinegrowers. Each year, the ceremony is held at a different wine village, in one or other of the viticultural areas in Burgundy, except Beaujolais which has its own celebrations.

After many celebrations in the chosen village (these include the Mass of Saint-Vincent and the procession of the Grand Council of the Order), participants re-assemble at Clos de Vougeot for an additional Chapter during which old servants of the vine are honoured.

The Confrérie des Chevaliers du Tastevin also patronises the *Tastevinage*, made up of gourmet judges who select the best wines submitted by growers and merchants. The selected wines are then permitted to carry a special label recognising their reward.

Finally, nearly every year since 1949, the Brotherhood of the Chevaliers du Tastevin have awarded a literary prize to a work or an author.

C) THE PAULÉE DE MEURSAULT (1)

Meursault, "capital of the great white wines of Burgundy", had the honour, after the last war, to re-establish the banquet which used to mark the end of the Harvest in days gone by, bringing the vineyard owners and the harvesters round the same table.

Actually, the Paulée de Meursault now brings people together who wish to meet in a friendly atmosphere. It is always held at midday on the Monday, the day after the wine sales of the Hospices de Beaune.

Each guest must bring along his own bottles of wine and more than twelve per square yard have been counted. The verve and high spirits of the Burgundians are freely aired during the joyful meal.

A literary prize of 100 bottles of Meursault is presented each year to the best work on French country life. Amongst the prize winners, one can pick out the names of Gaston Roupnel,

---

(1) All enquiries should be addressed to the Mairie de Meursault (Côte-d'Or) (80) 21.22.62.

Paul Cazin, Raymond Dumay, Colette, La Varende, Arnaud de Pesquidoux, Jean Bonnerot, Jean Robinet, Marie Noël, etc.

For some years now, the prize has been presented to a writer of repute even if their works only have a remote taste of the local soil.

Here are the prizewinner from 1973 to 1986 : Robert Sabatier, Alain Decaux, Gérard Oury, Christine Arnothy, Henri Vincenot, Pierre Bonte, Jean d'Ormesson, Guy des Cars, Maurice Denuzière, André Castelot, Claude Michelet, Yves Courrière.

2. FEW WINE SOCIETIES

A) Les Piliers Chablisiens (1)

At Chablis, "the Golden gateway of Burgundy", there is a Wine Brotherhood called "Les Piliers Chablisiens".

This Brotherhood was formed to honour all French and foreign personalities, but Burgundian at heart, who by their actions, written work or example, serve or have served the cause of Burgundy and, in particular, the Chablis vineyards, their wines, their spirit and their traditions.

The Chapters, during which new Piliers join the Brotherhood are held twice a year, in May on the feast of Saint-Cochon and at the end of November during the Exhibition and Tasting of the Wines from the Yonne.

A candlelight gastronomic luncheon precedes the reunion of each Chapter. Distinguished folklore entertainers embellish this banquet with their songs and dances.

B) The Cousinerie de Bourgogne

Based on legendary Burgundian hospitality "La Cousinerie de Bourgogne" was officially founded at Savigny-lès-Beaune on the 22nd January 1960, bearing as its motto "Gentle-

---

(1) All enquiries should be addressed to Les Piliers Chablisiens, Chablis (Yonne).

men are always cousins". It was on the occasion of the fête of Saint-Vincent that the original members found themselves surrounded by their first cousins dedicated to the birth of a great banquet in the communal cellars.

Nowadays, these new Cousins, whether they be Swiss, Belgian, Dutch or French, promise on their honour before their Chief and his Majordomo and other officers, all dressed in their old-fashioned costumes of gentlemen of the xviiith century, that they will practice Burgundian hospitality accepting in homage a "drop of blood" from their newly adopted soil, represented by the contents of dusty wine flagons. After this "consecration" they are awarded diplomas as proof of entry into their new-found family.

C) The Confrérie des Vignerons de Saint-Vincent at Mâcon (1)

This Brotherhood sits at Mâcon and has met since 1951. It took over from a Brotherhood of long standing in the village, which was on the point of disappearing and instilled a new lease of life into it.

"Chapters" are held during which new "chevaliers" or officers are received. These people are individuals who are considered worthy of this honour and of becoming both in France and throughout the world, supporters and ambassadors for the wines of Southern Burgundy.

---

(1) All enquiries should be addressed to the : Maison du tourisme de Mâcon, avenue De Lattre-de-Tassigny, tél. (85) 38.20.15.

"The honour of such a title cannot be bought, it can only be earned", so say the Brotherhood. During the enrolment ceremony, the "Matiscona" group sing the old songs of the ancient brotherhood of which one is a beautiful hymn to Saint-Vincent.

D) The Compagnons du Beaujolais

Now it happened that because a famous meeting took place shortly after Chrismas in 1947 in Eclair near Villefranche, the chief town of Beaujolais, a Brotherhood was formed, whose members bore the title of Compagnons du Beaujolais.

This is how several Beaujolais bred men founded the brotherhood whose aim is to promote the beauty and riches of their ancient Province.

The ceremony of initiation used to be held in a cellar in front of the statue of saint Vincent, either at the *Maison du Beaujolais* or at the Château de Pizay, Romanèche or elsewhere ; the Compagnons being dressed in their quaint and colourful costumes. To-day the companions are at home in a cellar owned by them at Lacenas.

The brotherhood organises, amongst others, a summer fête in a Beaujolais Communal wine Centre, a winter fête and "The Beaujolais Night" at the Palais de la Méditerranée at Nice.

"Exiled" compatriots in Paris have also founded with equal enthusiasm the *Devoir Parisien des Compagnons du Beaujolais* who combine their own efforts with that of the brotherhood to promote his region, and its wines.

3. OTHER FESTIVALS, FETES
OR REGIONAL FAIRS

A) THE WINE SALE OF THE HOSPICES
OF NUITS-SAINT-GEORGES

The Hospices of Nuits-Saint-Georges also has vineyards totaling about 12 hectares of first growths appellations.

Its production is commercialized every year the first sunday before Palm Sunday during a public auction. Less prestigious than Beaune's auction, the wine sale of the Hospices of Nuits-Saint-Georges is always a great success for the professionals of the area because of the quality of the wine.

The help given to the Hospices by this sales is used for the transformation and amelioration of a retirement home for the elderly. It is a perpetuation of a social tradition started in 1633 by Guillaume Labye, the king's procurator.

B) THE TASTEVINAGE

For more than thirty years the "Confrérie des Chevaliers du Tastevin" has decided to promote the quality of the great wines of Burgundy by creating the "Tastevinage".

Every year in the Spring the Confrérie asks a jury of about 160 persons, wellknown for their tasting tallent, to come to the Château du Clos de Vougeot. This jury selects the wine representing the best of the claimed appellation and vintage from among bottles presented anonymously by Burgundian winegrowers and wine merchants.

The selected wine get a special numbered label with the seal of the Confrérie and the labels are given to the proprietor of the wine for the exact quantity of bottles produced.

C) The International Exhibition of Food Wines and Gastronomy

Founded at Dijon after the Great War, by the former Minister Gaston Gerard, and known for a long time as the "Foire Gastronomique", it has continually expanded and developed. It became the International Exhibition of Food, Wines and Gastronomy and remains one of the biggest events in our region.

It is always held at the beginning of November.

Every two years (uneven years) in April, it organises the S.I.V.A. : The International Salon of Wines and Food which alternates with the S.I.A.L. at Paris (even years).

D) The National Wine Fair at Mâcon

This is held in the middle of the Spring. In addition to showing wines from the whole of Burgundy, it also offers a very large selection of wines coming from other regions of France which enthusiasts may taste.

E) The Table-Wine Fair of Chagny

Organised in the middle of August at Chagny (Saône-et-Loire), it allows enthusiasts to taste all the wines produced in the northern part of the Saône-et-Loire, and the regional appellations in particular : Bourgogne, Bourgogne Passe-Tout Grains, Bourgogne Aligoté, etc.

F) The Raclet Festival

Around 1840, the pyralis moth devastated the vineyards. It was Bernard Raclet of Romanèche who found and showed the benefits of treating the vines before growth began in the Spring.

His name is remembered each year towards the end of October by the Exhibition and Wine Market of the Mâconnais-Beaujolais, better known under the name of the Raclet Festival. The Beaujolais Nouveau celebrations are also combined with this festival.

G) The General Exhibition
of the Wines of Burgundy (1)

This Exhibition is organised in Beaune, at the same time as the general celebrations of the sale of wines belonging to the Hospice de Beaune. A great number of wines coming from

---

(1) Information : Secrétariat des Associations Viticoles, 20, place Monge, Beaune.

Burgundy are put on show for two days. It is possible to taste old wines as well as the new vintage.

A jury of qualified personalities takes advantage of the many samples to give their opinion on the new vintage.

H) THE WINE MUSEUM OF BURGUNDY

The wine lover who is interested in anything connected with wine and the vine will be fascinated when he visits the Musée du Vin de Bourgogne found in the former Hôtel des Ducs de Bourgogne (1).

A collection of stained glass windows showing the evolution and culture of the vine are beautifully presented by the curators of the Musée des Arts et Traditions Populaires de Paris. Every aspect covering the production and handling of wine is on show.

The Hôtel des Ducs de Bourgogne is another centre of the Ambassadeurs du Vin de France, founded by M. Duchet, former Mayor of Beaune and a former minister. The Ambassadeurs du Vin are chosen from élite personalities connected with the literary, political, military, industrial or commercial world, who actively advertise the virtues of the Wines of France.

* * *

(1) Visit with guide, everyday.

From all these societies and vinous festivities we have chosen the most lively and outstanding ones. It must be pointed out that their purpose is to advertise the wines of the region. But if they survive and if a number of them expand to the point where others copy their activities, it is because they hold a winning card : MONSEIGNEUR LE VIN DE BOURGOGNE, *the wine which asks the world to drink to the health of France.*

APPENDIX

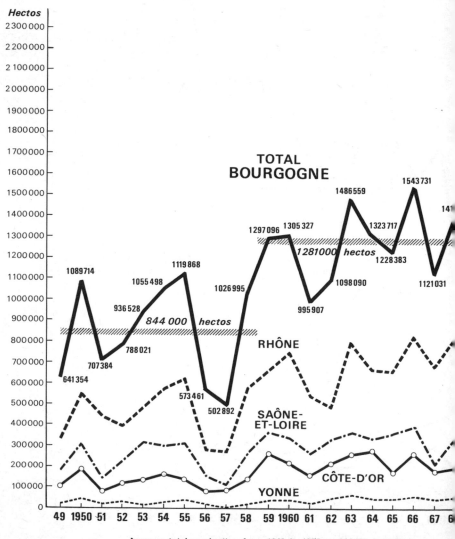

Hectos

TOTAL BOURGOGNE

1543731

1486559

141

1297096 1305327

1323717

1281000 hectos

1119868

1055498

1228383

1026995

1089714

936528

1098090

844 000 hectos

995907

788021

1121031

707384

RHÔNE

641354

573461

502892

SAÔNE-ET-LOIRE

CÔTE-D'OR

YONNE

49 1950 51 52 53 54 55 56 57 58 59 1960 61 62 63 64 65 66 67 6

Average total production from 1949 to 1958 : 844 171 hectolitres
Average total production from 1959 to 1968 : 1 281 186 hectolitres

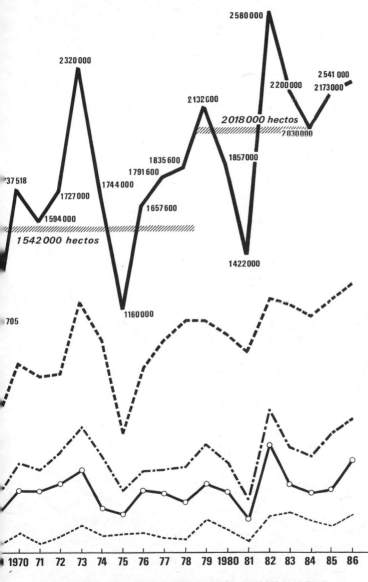

2580000

2320000

2541000
2200000   2173000

2132600
2018000 hectos
2030000

37518   1835600   1857000
1791600
1727000   1744000
1594000   1657600
1542000 hectos

1422000

705   1160000

1970 71 72 73 74 75 76 77 78 79 1980 81 82 83 84 85 86

Average total production from 1969 to 1978 : 1 542 209 hectolitres
Average total production from 1979 to 1986 : 2 117 000 hectolitres

LIST OF ALL COUNTRIES IMPORTING A.O.C. WINES FROM BURGUNDY IN 1986

with an indication of the imported volume and the value

EUROPE	Volume (in hecto)	Value (000's FF)
Allemagne fédérale...................	191 354	386 275
Allemagne démocratique	183	268
Andorre	257	495
Autriche	3 698	11 100
Belgo-Luxemb. (U.E.)	84 189	223 562
Danemark..........................	28 170	60 475
Finlande	4 428	13 001
Grande-Bretagne	191 648	579 395
Espagne	294	1 138
Irlande (Rép. d')	5 220	18 460
Islande	865	2 655
Italie	3 572	10 258
Norvège............................	6 584	13 593
Pays-Bas	72 447	160 151
Suède	16 446	42 602
Suisse	245 497	540 471

FRENCH TERRITORIES		
Guadeloupe	2 611	6 642
Guyane française	782	1 382
Martinique.........................	1 404	3 171
Nouvelle-Calédonie	1 395	3 410
Polynésie française	1 263	2 618
Réunion	1 302	2 567

	Volume (in hecto)	Value (000's FF)
AMERICA		
Antilles néerlandaises	446	2 128
Bahamas...........................	347	2 041
Bermudes..........................	764	4 118
Brésil	2 798	8 712
Canada	57 737	132 959
Barbade	257	1 324
Dominicaine	219	1 127
Etats-Unis	219 368	820 540
Mexique	603	3 800
Panama	277	1 329
Venezuela..........................	178	1 035
NEAR EAST		
Abu Dhabi	212	954
Bahrein...........................	395	1 478
Dubai.............................	451	1 925
Djibouti	162	287
Oman	172	592
AFRICA		
Afrique du Sud (Rép. d')	154	994
Bénin	232	444
Cameroun	1 241	2 471
Congo	274	626
Côte-d'Ivoire (Rép.)	1 969	4 534
Gabon	712	1 612
Centrafrique	116	280
Guinée	137	304
Maurice	108	234
Sénégal (Rép.)	435	963
Togo (Rép.)	316	773

ASIA AND THE SOUTH SEA ISLANDS	Volume (in hecto)	Value (000's FF)
Australie...............................	4 652	15 137
Corée du Sud	262	1 393
Hong-Kong	4 287	24 061
Indonésie	138	615
Japon	21 571	92 331
Nouvelle-Zélande	565	2 244
Singapour...........................	1 918	7 859
Thaïlande...........................	951	3 378
Malaisie	536	2 063

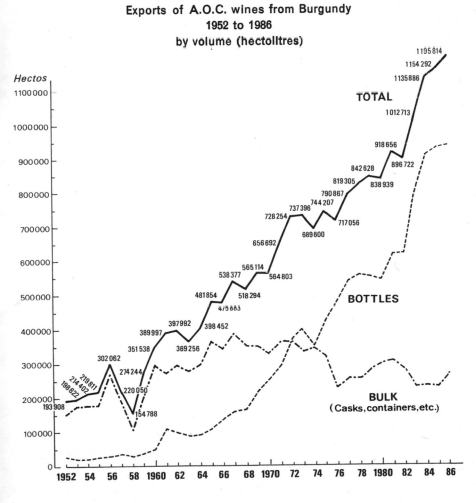

Exports of A.O.C. wines from Burgundy
1952 to 1986
by volume (hectolitres)

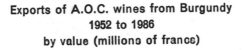

Exports of A.O.C. wines from Burgundy
1952 to 1986
by value (millions of francs)

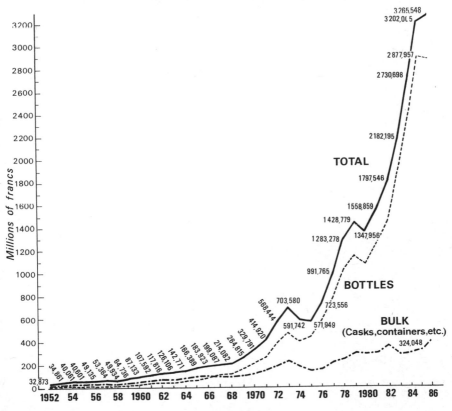

INDEX

I N D E X

Some useful information

INTERPROFESSIONAL COMMITTEES

The three interprofessional Committees below are always ready
to give all the information they have about the wines and the cellars
of the regions which concern them :

— C.I.B. (Comité Interprofessionnel de la Côte-d'Or et de l'Yonne
pour les Vins de Bourgogne), rue Henri-Dunan, 21200 Beaune,
tél. 80.22.21.35 ;

— C.I.B.M. (Comité Interprofessionnel de Saône-et-Loire pour les
Vins A.O.C. de Bourgogne et de Mâcon), Maison du Tourisme,
avenue de Lattre-de-Tassigny, 71000 Mâcon, tél. 85.38.20.15 ;

— U.I.V.B. (Union Interprofessionnelle des Vins du Beaujolais),
210, bd Vermorel, 69400 Villefranche-sur-Saône, tél. 74.65.45.55.

BIBLIOGRAPHY

DANGUY (R.) et AUBERTIN (Ch.). — *Les grands vins de Bourgogne* (Dijon, 1892). (Réimpression par Laffitte Reprints, Marseille, 1978.)

DUMAY (R.), BAZIN (J.-F.), BERNARD (R.), GERRIET (L.), GOUZE (R.) et POUPON (P.). — *Le vin de Bourgogne* (Ed. Montalba, 1976).

DUYKER (H.). — *Grands vins de Bourgogne* (Nathan, Paris, 1980).

FERRÉ (L.). — *Traité d'œnologie bourguignonne* (I.N.A.O., 1958).

GADILLE (R.). — *Le vignoble de la côte bourguignonne* (Belles-Lettres, Paris, 1967).

LANDRIEU-LUSSIGNY (M.-H.). — *Le vignoble bourguignon, ses lieux-dits* (Jeanne Laffitte, Marseille, 1983).

LÉGLISE (M.). — *Principes de vinification* (Comité interprofessionnel de Bourgogne, Beaune, 1969).

— *Elevage et conservation du vin en cave* (Comité interprofessionnel de Bourgogne, Beaune, 1974).

— *Une initiation à la dégustation des grands vins* (Divo, Lausanne, 1976).

ORIZET (L.). — *Les vins de France* (Presses Universitaires de France).

QUITTANSON (Ch.) et VANHOUTTE (R.). — *La protection des appellations d'origine et le commerce des vins et eaux-de-vie* (Ed. Journée vinicole).

RODIER (C.). — *Le vin de Bourgogne* (Damidot-Dijon).

ROUPNEL (G.). — *La Bourgogne* (Horizons de France).

ROZET (G.). — *La Bourgogne, tastevin en main* (Horizons de France).

Imprimé en France
Imprimerie des Presses Universitaires de France
73, avenue Ronsard, 41100 Vendôme
Novembre 1987 — N° 33 306